WHY
LABELLE
MATTERS

M Music
M Matters

Evelyn McDonnell and Oliver Wang

Series Editors

WHY LABELLE MATTERS

Adele Bertei

UNIVERSITY OF TEXAS PRESS
AUSTIN

Requests for permission to reproduce material from this work should be sent to:
Permissions
University of Texas Press
P.O. Box 7819
Austin, TX 78713-7819
utpress.utexas.edu/rp-form

♾ The paper used in this book meets the minimum requirements of ANSI/NISO
Z39.48-1992 (R1997) (Permanence of Paper).

Library of Congress Cataloging-in-Publication Data

Names: Bertei, Adele, author.
Title: Why Labelle matters / Adele Bertei.
Other titles: Music matters.
Description: First edition. | Austin : University of Texas Press, 2021.
| Series: Music matters | Includes bibliographical references.
Identifiers:
LCCN 2020043588
ISBN 978-1-4773-2040-2 (paperback)
ISBN 978-1-4773-2289-5 (library ebook)
ISBN 978-1-4773-2290-1 (ebook)
Subjects: LCSH: Labelle (Musical group) | LaBelle, Patti. | Hendryx, Nona.
| Dash, Sarah. | Wickham, Vicki. | Girl groups (Musical groups)—United States.
| Music and race—United States. | Sex in music | Afrofuturism.
Classification: LCC ML421.L33 B23 2021 | DDC 782.42166092/2 [B]—dc23
LC record available at https://lccn.loc.gov/2020043588

doi:10.7560/320402

for ECSG
and spacegirls throughout the galaxies

CONTENTS

PREFACE

Labelle: the beautiful. Say the name Labelle and most neural pathways lead straight to Patti LaBelle, diva extraordinaire—as if Labelle, the entity of three, never were. The first all-woman band of rock stars to grace our planet, Labelle were three artists and a silent fourth who, across two decades and seventeen years together, created a legacy unlike that of any other music group before or since. Patti's miraculous voice led the way, undoubtedly. But it was Sarah Dash's vivacious personality and sweet soprano, Nona Hendryx's deeply resonant voice and fiery imagination, and futurist manager Vicki Wickham's vision that would ultimately result in the creation of the Labellian cosmology—a space-time map of sonic starlight.

The first group to break away from the traditional girl-group matrix of the 1960s, Labelle reinvented themselves into a thrilling Other. Tired of trying to fit in, they chose to stand out by mixing their gospel roots with electrifying funk, rock, and sounds of New Orleans, topped with lyrics voicing truth to power. Theirs was a banquet of Black female rebellion audiences had been waiting to feast on.

Provoked by manager Vicki Wickham, the bouffant wigs and chiffon girl-group dresses were tossed onto the pyre as Patti, Nona, and Sarah danced over the flames in space-age sartorial glam. Labelle's musical juju brought them all the way from playing the sardine houses of the Chitlin' Circuit to headlining New York City's Metropolitan Opera House; they were the first contemporary music act and Black female vocal group to perform at the Met. Labelle's carnal sonic combustion on "Lady Marmalade" brought a New Orleans hooker into nearly every home, club, and corner shop around the world. Americans learned to speak their first words of *français*-funk courtesy of Labelle, some unaware they were reciting an invitation to *se faire baiser* via "Voulez-vous coucher avec moi, ce soir?" Patti, Nona, and Sarah channeled Lady M.'s erotic ferocity in the spirit of Ralph Ellison's "Change the Joke and Slip the Yoke," blowing up the racist Jezebel stereotype by flaunting their sexual agency with the roar of a three-headed lioness.

The LP *Nightbirds* invited us to board the original Mothership, giving pre–Dr. Funkenstein, goddess-style Afronautica in sound and vision. Their music remains a clarion call. To rise above the hypocrisies of American life on the wings of music. To soar into a compassionate and funky galaxy of love-sexy liberation. Their presentation was brand-ass new, brand-spanking funky, and divinely erotic.

Labelle sang the opening aria of Afrofuturism. Aside from the most apparent mentions—Octavia Butler, Alice Coltrane—the absence of woman, of her voice in the majority of man-texts on Afrofuturism, is bewildering. Women like Alondra Nelson and Ytasha L. Womack have stepped in to course-correct as important theorists on

Afrofuturism and the role Black women have played in its shaping. Thanks to Womack's brilliant primer on Afrofuturism, I've discovered Nalo Hopkinson and N. K. Jemison (writers of speculative and science fiction), and Afua Richardson, the illustrator who gave us *Black Panther: World of Wakanda*. If we imagine the presence of ghosts snapping the rubber bands of space and time, might Toni Morrison be thought of as an Afrofuturist? There's a series of photographs by Waring Abbott of a glowing Morrison dancing at a disco in 1974. I'd wager a bet she's dancing to the liberating funk of a track Labelle released that year called "Goin' on a Holiday." "Heading for the hills, where I know I'm not the hunted prey."

Does the female voice, at the height of its erotic power in/on the body and its ability to soar through skins and time, scare the male intellect into its omission?

Sunday, February 16, 1975—A Journey Backward

I'm standing in the lobby of an opulent jewel box built in the 1920s: Cleveland's Allen Theater. Designed in the Italian Renaissance style to resemble Rome's Villa Madama, the dramatic venue is a match for what will be one of the most extraordinary theatrical experiences of my life. I take in the room and the excitable crowd on parade, all following the advertised edict of the *Nightbirds* show to "Wear Something Silver." If your spaceship happened to land here this night, you'd never imagine Cleveland as segregated; the two-thousand-plus crowd is equally mixed, and the only tension I feel is the anticipation of the show we're about to witness. Silver-clad bodies pose, connect, laugh. Admire one another coiffed in mylar, shiny satin, sequined tulle, silver-sprayed leather, and platinum jewelry fit for Venetian and Caribbean Carnival. A gent in white leather chaps cupping silver-painted butt cheeks saunters past a gorgeous young androgyne, face smeared in hot pink and speckled with stars. They bump into me, blow a kiss. I see smiles of admiration for metallic blue complementing silver antennae on an Amazonian space queen. I'm sporting DIY silver cuffs and an Egyptian-style collar, both fashioned out of tin foil and cardboard. My blue satin hot pants, silver glitter platforms, and orange mullet are holdovers from Bowie's *Diamond Dogs* floor show, June of 1974. The Black fantastic was not in attendance for the Bowie show, but tonight is a celebration of a new and different hue.

As the ushers ring the curtain bell, bodies rush, misting the floor with silver dust. The lights dim, but none of us can sit, nerves wound tight with anticipation . . . and then, a piano, intro notes playing softly as a circle of light grows to reveal a woman-creature inside its glow. She's covered in alien space-age suiting and feathers, alone in the spotlight. Sarah begins to sing high and pure, "Nightbird fly by the light of the moon . . . she's flying high and all alone." Suddenly, to Sarah's right, night-bird Nona descends from above on wires, an Afronaut deity from space touching down to join Sarah in a cradle of warm harmony, returning from a galaxy unknown. We catch our collective breath as another body, a winged creature, emerges from on high. Nearly concealed in a cage made of trembling feathers, a wingspread capable of enfolding us all begins to unfurl to reveal Patti. When she alights onto the stage and turns to face us, the three lock their voices into harmony and the crowd erupts.

I was taking in two shows that night: Labelle's revolutionary performance onstage and the elation of the audience around me, an integration so foreign to the city yet so perfectly held in the embrace of Labelle's music. This was an experience of sound and vision expressing what Martin Luther King Jr. spoke of as our "inescapable network of mutuality."

Not only did Labelle bring the feelings and the glam, they gave us outer-limits sexuality. Watching spacegirls Labelle flirt with girl-on-girl action was an extreme high for this queer girl. When Nona started chasing Sarah around the stage with a whip, I nearly had a seizure. Were any of Labelle's divas actually queer? There were rumors. I guess it comes down to our singular interpretations of identity politricks and the art of labeling. Or in Nona's case, *un*labeling. (She remains notoriously private.) Labelle magnified the fierce love my queer friends and I had kept tamped down for too long, the joy we couldn't express aching there beneath the shame society had beaten into us. That night we were shame-free. Dancing with each other, showing off our moves while drinking in the eye candy onstage and all around us. We were Labelle's "Space Children."

When the concert ended, I ran outside to the back alley of the theater and found Labelle's limousine waiting. The three singers and their manager exited the backstage door and I stepped out of the shadows, nearly paralyzed with admiration. Caught in their headlights, I vaguely remember them laughing—not in a mean way, more in surprised acknowledgment of a little glitterbug androgyne. Patti asked, "Are you a boy or a girl?" Shaking, I answered, "Um, both?" More laughter, the good kind. I mustered up the courage to say it was the best show I'd ever seen. They thanked me, climbed into the limo, and pulled away, while I stood rooted to the spot, freezing the moment in time forever.

Why Labelle Matters is the story of an all-girl band riding a cultural roller coaster together across the decades while singing their power over every steep ascent and dip. How did they do it? How did Labelle manage to claim their space as such unique women artists in a time when male heteronormative dictates held a near stranglehold on the presentation of women entertainers? Here one arrives at a fundamental theory of why Labelle matters: they succeeded, not by visionary talent and stamina alone, but by fiercely protecting their core strength: *their union with one another.* The power of a group of women—in this case, of Black and white and straight and queer women working together—dedicated to creating something of cultural import was chimeric in the early 1970s. The very concept of women working together across race, class, and the sharp borders of identity continues to require the imagining of a world different from where we live today. What Patti, Nona, Sarah, and Vicki (their manager) created together was utopian. Decidedly, and beautifully, feminist, the Labelle project pointed the way to possibilities shimmering on the edge of our horizon.

I'm a white queer woman lucky enough to have found Labelle when I needed them most—as a teenager having barely survived a childhood that defies belief. I spent several teenage years incarcerated, where my skin color was in the minority and gospel music was the go-to for soothing the traumas I shared with the Blossom Hill girl choir. (We were hardly *hoodlum*, although we fronted as if we were. Abandonment often lands kids in juvenile jails when they can't be contained elsewhere.) Most white working people, including my family, would never experience the close company of Black working people. In the ethos of divide and conquer, we have nearly three centuries of white politicians maintaining American segregation to thank for our divisions, as well as the lies we've been taught about our American history. As for the scuffles around race that sometimes occurred in these juvie institutions? Music was a wise referee. When we were singing side by side I felt only the camaraderie of voices and notes, and through song, trauma eased. The women and girls of Blossom Hill were my family, and music, the glue capable of pulling fractures into bone-strong wholeness.

Some forty years later as I reflect backward, I understand more about why I connected with Labelle's music
so profoundly: why Labelle matters *to me*, and why their
story cries out for recognition and honor. Listen today
and Labelle songs *still* hold. Soothe. Lift. Pull you into a
love-sexy dance of liberation. Through a mix of research,
interviews, my own personal experiences, and my passion for the music, I offer this telling of Labelle's story.
May it prove not only illuminating about the group but
also inspiring as to how music can heal, build bridges, and
transform culture.

WHY
LABELLE
MATTERS

— 1 —

CHURCH:
AVIARY OF THE GIRL-CHILD

Some kids run away from home to get away from it all.
I had nowhere to run. So I took flight in song.

PATTI LABELLE

Every disease is a musical problem; every cure
is a musical solution.

NOVALIS, quoted by Oliver Sacks

The song of Labelle begins in the aviary, the church, where gospel music teaches Black girls how to fly.[1] Church is sanctuary, is cultural womb to Black music. And despite the Black church's patriarchal and homophobic bent (hardly unique when it comes to organized religions), the majority of celebrated voices leading the charge to aural holiness belong to women. Tap many a magnificent singer—from Mahalia to Aretha, Dionne Warwick to Patti LaBelle, Whitney Houston to Jennifer Hudson—and you'll find the double helix of gospel music and faith winding up the backbone of her DNA. I sang gospel for several years of my life and can attest to the feeling it brings; in a gospel choir you are carried by the voices inside and around you, goading you to soar with the promise that be you joyful or feeling broken, upon return, a lifeboat of bulletproof harmonics will be waiting to row you ashore. In such holosonic presence, only a cement block would not be moved, and this too is questionable.[2]

Young Patsy (Patti) Holt heard the call to music in the mid-1950s. She began showing off in the Young Adults Choir at Beulah Baptist Church in South Philly, which would prove to be a healing antidote to traumas she was experiencing as a pubescent girl. In her memoir, *Don't Block the Blessings*, Patti speaks wistfully about singing with her father and singing solos in church, encouraged by choir director Harriet Chapman, who warned how she'd better recognize her voice as a precious gift from God and directed Patti to "use it, don't lose it."

When Patti listened to her brother Junior's jazz records—vocalists like Sarah Vaughan, Dinah Washington, Gloria Lynne, Nina Simone, and Dakota Staton—the effect of these women's voices was revelatory. Not only did she discover the mirror of her teenage yearnings about love; she was listening to the kind of women she longed to be. She'd stand in a mirror, posing with a broom handle, singing her face off, all the while learning how the voice can channel and release the storm of emotions swirling inside a girl. The voice, that power vibrating from diaphragm to chest, through heart and head. Released to soar on air.

I hear Gloria Lynne's style as sounding closest to Patti's because of its raw, emotional reach. Lynne's voice will take you on a steady ride through a song and then, BAM, out leaps a dramatic surprise attack as she begins to riff. Listen to "I'm Glad There Is You," where Lynne defies gravity and the vocal booth, just as Patti would in later years. You can say Patti Holt had a calling. At the root of the word *vocation* is *vox*, Latin for "voice," and *vocare*, for "calling." Vocation isn't necessarily religious in scope—it's what you feel called to do, why you've manifested here on this mortal coil. The book of John starts, "In the beginning was the word, and the word was with God and the word was God." I see it this way: In the beginning was the word, and word is sound, is wave and vibration of a bang some thirteen billion years ago, setting all into motion. Stephon Alexander's *The Jazz of Physics* brings the science, laying out how the behavior of the cosmos is based in music—the Pythagorean "music of the spheres."[3]

Patti stepped out for her first solo in the church choir at twelve years old, her talent bringing the house to a standing ovation. Twelve was a pivotal age, and 1956, a loaded year for Patti. There was violence between her parents, and in her memoir she bravely reveals being sexually abused by one of her mother's boyfriends. In case one imagines "music as medicine" to be hyperbole (and as a survivor of trauma myself), singing is a balm capable of soothing, if not outright healing, the darkest of wounds.

In the geography of health, the vagus nerve is the largest

nerve in our bodies, connecting to our vocal cords and the muscles at the back of the throat. *Vagus* comes from the Latin word for "wandering," and true to its root, the nerve flows from the brain stem like a river, branching out into tributaries that roam throughout the body, connecting to its most vital organs: brain, heart, stomach, lungs. When the vagus nerve is compromised, all manner of illness can result. It is the primary controller of our parasympathetic nervous system, counterpoint to the "fight or flight" responses of the sympathetic nervous system, where trauma lives and thrives. One of several actions to keep the vagus nerve toned and healthy is singing, and singing releases oxytocin, known as the "love hormone." The social interaction and neurochemistry of choral singing and its ability to raise endorphin levels is currently a major focus of scientific inquiry, especially in the realm of healing trauma.[4]

Enslaved Africans brought call-and-response singing to the plantations, which morphed into work songs, praise songs, and spirituals. Besides the effect of emotional bonding, group singing had a very physical effect on Black bodies and minds suffering the horrors of slavery. A research study in 2013 demonstrated how singing lifted the depression of its test subjects substantially, apparent in brain scans before and after singing with a choir.[5] All this to say that Patti discovered the medicine capable of healing her wounds, washing the hurt away with vibrational waves of sonic joy. One day, she and her choirgirl sisters in Labelle would deliver the cure to all those captured by their music.

Nona Hendryx sang in her church choir as a teenager because, she tells me, "It's a Black thing, and expected of girls."[6] She fondly recalls the inspirational voice of Mrs. Wade, head of her church choir at Grant Chapel AME in Trenton, New Jersey. Nona, the nerd of Labelle, preferred hitting the books, not imagining music as a vocation but loving it nonetheless. In her memoir, Patti says Nona speaks of her youth as being "stone ghettoite." The nerd I discovered was more interested in Shakespeare than in hitting the streets, more drawn to archery and tennis at Trenton Central High. Young Nona loved poets Robert Frost and Emily Dickinson. She envisioned a future as a teacher of English, maybe history. She wrote her first poems at fifteen.

TV shows of the 1950s and '60s were rife with outer space themes, and Nona recalls being fascinated by Buster Crabbe as Flash Gordon conquering Mars. Shows like *Science Fiction Theatre* and *The Twilight Zone* and the revenge story of *Attack of the 50 Foot Woman* provided childhood inspirations that would spark future lyrics. These jejune sci-fi stories also provoked the imagination of literary witch and Afrofuturist Octavia Butler, who claimed that a B movie called *Devil Girl from Mars* launched her toward authorship with the epiphany, "Gee, I can write a better story than *that*!"[7]

Growing up, Nona listened to doo-wop groups the Drifters and Little Anthony and the Imperials, and to early rock and roll singers like Chuck Berry. Most teenage girls in the

1950s wouldn't have been aware of the birth mothers of rock and roll, Sister Rosetta Tharpe and Big Mama Thornton, unless they knew music aficionados and record collectors among friends and family. More than five decades later here we are, finally recognizing the tremendous impact of Tharpe and Thornton as root creators of rock and roll. It's Elvis Presley's "Hound Dog" Nona remembers grooving to, not Big Mama's. (Big Mama's "Hound Dog" was number one on the R&B charts for several weeks in 1952, when Patti, Nona, and Sarah would have been around seven or eight years old.) Chuck Berry's "Maybellene" and Sam Cooke were also favorites, performers who eventually became Labelle's contemporaries on the Chitlin' Circuit.

A calling can arise at any time, and Nona heard it distinctly when first blending her voice with the voices of the women bound to share her destiny. Their sweet vocal communion became the lure beckoning Nona toward a path as singer, songwriter, and, one day, world creator.

Sarah Dash opened up to sing with the choir one day in second grade, surprising all in attendance. She's the seventh of thirteen children in a tight-knit family, daughter of an elder and pastor in the Pentecostal Trinity Church of Christ (also in Trenton). Pastors are leaders of their communities, men who do not want their daughters entertaining thoughts of hitting the road to sing in juke joints. Says Sarah: "If you sing the devil's music, you do devilish things. Black young girls, any young girls being on the road, well, people heard things. But I would say to them [her parents], 'You know how you raised me.'"[8] Sarah is in good company with many other singers born of pastor fathers: Aretha, Darlene Love, and Merry Clayton, among others. And like Patti, young Sarah was taken over by the power and grace of singing. She accepted the call to gift people with her voice. Eventually, her family would witness Labelle in a formidable moment of their career, and on that fateful night, Pentecostal reservations would dissolve as Sarah's proud parents applauded her gifts.

Sarah's need to sing soon blossomed into the dream of a girl group of her very own. She knew it wasn't enough to sing beautifully, and wanted more for the music. What lies at the root of the song? What is the broken spirit or the joy inside lifting the notes, notes that can carry a listener to new places in space-time? She listened for the answers in church, and on the radio, in the singers she adored: Johnny Mathis and Andy Williams, Mahalia Jackson, Gladys Knight, Smokey Robinson, Sarah Vaughan, Carmen McRae, doo-woppers the Capris, who hit with "There's a Moon Out Tonight." As her voice matured she developed a full, sweet tone with a considerable range up top. Sarah's tone is rounder than Patti's or Nona's, and she has a stellar reach—nearly as Olympian as Patti's. Sarah's voice became the glue, the plus sign in the sonic equation we'd come to know as Labelle.

The day Sarah Dash's church choir visited Nona's church happened to be the day Nona subbed for another singer in the choir. Sarah heard the smooth, dusky-voiced Nona step out for her solo and instantly recognized the voice needed to complete her girl-group dream. Nona is often described as an alto; she definitely has the anchoring voice of the trio, but her substantial range qualifies her more as a mezzo-soprano. Nona's voice is like dusk on a summer's night. Her vocal timbre has a warm, sexy resonance; you can almost feel it reach out and wrap itself around you.

In the documentary about backing singers *20 Feet from Stardom*, singer Darlene Love explains how singing in church teaches you precisely where your voice belongs in harmony with others, how you learn where to slide in to the blend.[9] It's instinctual; nothing to do with reading musical notation. Sarah understands blend, maybe better than Nona and Patti. Nona tells me when the three get together to sing and the harmony doesn't sound right, Sarah is the one to point out the wayward note and the correction.

Sarah asked Nona to join her a cappella group the Del Capris, a name fashioned from slapping doo-wop's favorite prefix, Del, on to her favorite doo-wop group, the Capris. Forty miles away in Philly, radio signals were drawing Patsy Holt to the same Black stations dialed in by Nona and Sarah in Trenton. Station WHAT competed with WDAS, the "Sound of Philadelphia," featuring legendary disc jockeys like Hy Lit, Sonny Hopson, the "Ace from Outer Space" Jocko Henderson, and Georgie Woods (who would be among the first to play the Bluebelles in heavy rotation). These DJs spun great soul and R&B tunes, also using radio as a megaphone to inform their communities about the civil rights movement and the events and actions of the day. Patti got her temporal music high on from the girl groups she heard on the radio: the Chantels, the Chiffons, the Shirelles. She wanted in, so she pulled together a quartet of schoolmates and they sang wherever they could grab attention—at parties and dances, on porches, at bus stops—performing for whomever might listen.

In 1961, Patti's first singing group auditioned for manager and talent booker Bernard Montague and signed with him, calling themselves the Ordettes—but the Ordettes soon fell apart. Two of the girls chose to marry and have families, as did most young women in the 1960s. Patti attempted to perform solo, stepping up alone to the microphone in Montague's revues and proving she was capable of transfixing an audience with her voice. She had the goods but didn't enjoy performing on her own. Patti felt safer, soared higher on the wings of vocal camaraderie.

Coincidentally, Montague also signed our girls from Trenton—Nona and Sarah, the Del Capris—and a game of musical chairs commenced. Singers were often moved around by male Svengalis in a shuffleboard game ubiquitous to girl groups of the 1950s and '60s. There would be several iterations of singers before the group eventually materialized as the trio Labelle. In the case of the two Del Capris meeting the remaining Ordettes, it was a fortunate play for all.

I imagine the initial moment of Nona and Sarah meeting Patti and Sandra Tucker (the remaining Ordette);

the magic that happens when voices dance together. The shock on Nona's and Sarah's faces when Patti steps central, launching into "Somewhere Over the Rainbow." Patti takes a body and soul beyond the polychromic with her extraordinary voice, a range so impressive it flips the bird to octave seven. Patti, Nona, Sarah, and Sandra immersed themselves in long shifts of sweat-drenched rehearsals— harmony arrangements and choreographed steps practiced under the watchful eye of their beloved choreographer and arranger Morris "Mo" Bailey. Mo, who had created musical arrangements for Nina Simone and Curtis Mayfield, was Philly's equivalent to Detroit's Cholly Atkins, choreographer at the Motown charm school.

All signals flashed green for the group to hit the road until Sandra's folks slammed the brakes. They were not having their daughter quit school for a life on the road— *with musicians? Ha!* Montague put out the call for yet another new member, and in strolled Cindy Birdsong. She'd caught word from a friend of Montague's about a girl group in need of a singer. Cindy had the voice, the beauty, and the charm worthy of her surname. When the four sang together, they felt it immediately: kismet in the blend. The musical and personal chemistry the girls had been seeking was finally complete, and the quartet—Patti, Nona, Sarah, and Cindy—become the Bluebelles.

The Bluebelles fell prey to girl-group musical hijinks after signing their first recording deal with local wheeler-dealer Harold B. Robinson's label Newtown Records.

Robinson was in possession of another girl group's master, a song called "I Sold My Heart to the Junkman." The Bluebelles are credited on the 45's label as the artist, proxy for the real singers on the track, a group called the Starlets. Robinson released the track with the Starlets singing, and the Bluebelles began to promote the song live as it rose up the charts. But when the Starlets discovered their voices on the radio being credited to another singing group, all hell broke loose, sinking the record into legal quicksand. Robinson brought Patti, Nona, Cindy, and Sarah to the rescue, and they rerecorded the vocals. The new version sounded close enough to the original to pass, but better (Patti's in the house!). Jazzed by the glory of Bluebelle voices, Robinson was overcome by a delirium of belles. He named his new label Bluebelle Records but didn't stop there, renaming Patsy Holt as Patti *LaBelle*. Ironic, since Robinson had rejected Patti when he first laid eyes on her during the audition.

Patti recalls their initial meeting with Robinson: "And when we went to him, the first thing he said after seeing us is that I'm too Black and ugly, so he did not want to give us a chance. And so Montague, who was our manager at the time, said to Mr. Robinson, you need to hear them sing. So we did 'Danny Boy' or 'You'll Never Walk Alone,' and honey, all the Black and ugly left my face. . . . After that, he didn't see any more ugly, he didn't see any more Black; all he saw was green."[10] Robinson signed the act and christened Patti and the group, à la française, as Patti

LaBelle and the Bluebelles. He printed the run of "I Sold My Heart to the Junkman" with the Bluebelles on vocals, and the record kept climbing, hitting number fifteen on the pop charts. The Bluebells surfaced from Robinson's legal miasma unscathed, with their star on the rise.

Having a hit record creates a demand for live shows, and Montague needed the girls out on the road touring to support their hit, but there was a catch: they hadn't yet graduated from high school. Their families were sold on the idea of the group's success, but quitting school? Patti's mother felt confident in Patti's future as a star performer and was the first to grant permission for Patti to drop out. Nona and Sarah followed suit, but not without grief from their families. (Nona and Sarah studied and aced their GEDs while on the road, and later Patti earned an equivalency diploma from the high school of her teenage years.) All families insisted the girls travel with a chaperone and a tutor: manager Bernard Montague and his wife, who wisely packed heat, since driving while Black through the Deep South in the 1960s could get you killed. And a woman would be a less suspicious gunslinger if the car happened to be stopped by the Klan, the police, or a Klan-policeman, a conflation typical of the Jim Crow South.

Just as the Borscht Belt and its comedians and singers provided nourishment for East Coast Jews dealing with anti-Semitism in the 1940s, Black entertainers and entrepreneurs created a network of venues on a much larger scale, calling it the Chitlin' Circuit. The circuit's moniker has been attributed to Lou Rawls, but the name has everything to do with the pork scraps fed to antebellum slaves, elevated into a beloved staple of soul food. Yes, you can make a silk purse out of a sow's innards by adding the nourishment music provides.

Clubs, juke joints, and theaters scattered throughout the South and as far west as Texas became hot touring spots for Tina Turner, Chuck Berry, Little Richard, Gladys Knight, and most of the Black performers responsible for creating rhythm and blues, soul, and funk. Jimi Hendrix cut his teeth working the Chitlin' Circuit, as did comedians Moms Mabley, Pigmeat Markham, Shirley Hemphill, and LaWanda Page. Chitlin' Circuit entrepreneurs were equal opportunity employers when it came to gender and sexuality. (But just how free Little Richard, Moms Mabley, Bessie Smith, Ma Rainey, and others felt about being their authentic queer selves is a question demanding a deep dive of its own.) Accounts of murder and suicide (the infamous Russian roulette demise of Johnny Ace comes to mind), of racketeers, bootleggers, tough-ass women venue owners, and all manner of freely expressed sexual modalities—these sensational stories of Black culture are too often the focus of what DJ scholar Lynnée Denise calls the "pesky White gaze." The real gold of the Chitlin' Circuit story lies in its importance as America's first network of independent entertainment businesses and venues solely designed, owned, and operated by and for Black Americans. From roadside juke joints all the way to the Apollo Theater (white-owned at the time, but exclusively Black otherwise), the Chitlin' Circuit flourished during Jim Crow, providing a supportive business network for Black entertainers to perfect their craft. Mark Anthony Neal writes about the Chitlin' Circuit as possibly having been the "most critical site for the incubation of modern Black culture,"[11] noting how the civil rights movement took advantage of the circuit's established social networks to build connections nationwide.

"I Sold My Heart to the Junkman" won the Bluebelles an appearance on *American Bandstand*, and the Chitlin' Circuit provided the perfect performance school on their path toward success. But the racism they encountered on the road during Jim Crow was brutal. Patti tells a tale of one hellacious cross-country drive to Los Angeles from the East Coast that included having to back down from a near execution squad in a whites-only restaurant in Texas, only to discover too late that their take-out food had been poisoned. The same cross-country journey culminated in a meeting with James Brown. He brought the Bluebelles on tour as his opening act and lived to regret it when he heard the foot-stomping roar of their audiences demanding multiple encores. Patti recounts a night when the girls put on a spectacular performance and returned to the stage to greet their standing ovation. Brown demanded the curtains be slammed down on them midbow.

The Bluebelles presented in typical girl-group fashion and form, where coloring outside the lines was forbidden. They replicated the styles of their sister singers:

matching bouffant wigs often crowned with tiaras, gloves, ankle bracelets, and pumps, all identical except for variations in the colors of their dresses. They didn't have gown money, but the stage dresses they chose were stylish enough for Diana Ross to envy and copy. Gold lamé was their most risqué—"mermaid suits," Patti calls them—with tight pants showing some curve. For the most part, "We looked like matrons." she says. "We never wanted to look sexy." The demure girl groups were not about to take any chances. Not in rock, "not even in roll," states Patti.[12] She often tells the story of times when Miss Ross of the Supremes insinuated herself backstage at the Apollo while the Bluebelles were dressing, doling out compliments and charm. Upon discovering the Bluebelles were about to wear the same drag hanging in the Supremes' dressing room, Ross convinced the stage manager to let the Supremes go on first. The Bluebelles wondered, *Why would headliners the Supremes want to open for the Bluebelles?* The answer stung; the Supremes strolled out onstage in those very same outfits, making the Bluebelles look like copycats.

The Bluebelles' polished choreography mimicked the lyrical supplication of good girls singing about hetero love, their mannerisms, kitten meek. It's the fire in Patti's voice propelling the group off the assembly line, more apparent in their second hit, "Down the Aisle (The Wedding Song)." Patti waxes on about how blissful she and her man's wedding will be. Typical girl-group fare. But wait. There's something about the tonality of the backing harmonies . . .

and that voice on top, so incredibly confident, so powerful. Near the song's end, Patti hits a high note and holds it; for the musical nerds, a D#6 (two octaves above middle C). Patti takes on opera's stratospheric coloratura sopranos, using the whistle register of her voice. She was the first singer to employ the "whistle" voice in pop music, later to be eclipsed by Minnie Riperton and Mariah Carey. Patti's vocal acrobatics set the Bluebelles apart from other girl groups, breaking the lock on the genre's production jail by defying producers who didn't know how to handle a voice capable of blowing out studio speakers. But it was the particular quality of Nona's and Sarah's voices in concert with Patti's that made their group sound nonpareil. Nona's and Sarah's backing vocals were more than wallpaper to Patti's lead.

As early as 1963, the Bluebelles presented a show that demanded attention. Girl groups of the 1960s might have had singers painting pictures of dramatic street scenes (the Shangri-Las) or delivering infectious grooves that set an entire nation to dancing in the streets (Martha Reeves and the Vandellas), but none had the extraordinary voice and range of Patti. Patti LaBelle fans have most likely read reports of her cantankerous physicality, and she's the first person to claim her inner demon, "Priscilla," as someone you do not want to mess with. (Patti often talks about Priscilla, her pugilistic avatar who will jump you after one too many provocations.) But when it comes to music, sometimes a voice needs messing with to reach that much higher.

You can only be as good as the players on your team. Nona and Sarah knew precisely where to aim, hold, and cross the notes that tripped the switch to Patti's explosive delivery. I hear Priscilla in so many Labelle tracks (e.g., "Get You Somebody New" and "Isn't It a Shame"), battling it out with her musical soul mates in a launch toward Jupiter, each one on a path to outrun the other before joining back up to bring the team across the galactic finish line. Sometimes I hear Labelle singing so aggressively, they sound punk, as in *gospel punk*: the passion and heat of gospel, the ferocity and wild abandon of punk. The rawness of their three voices together create a sonic rage of love. Like the Apache dancers of fin de siècle Paris, it's all drama and mock roughnecking on a musical staff, a dance of hot beauty in conflict and release.

Here I must return to the power of gospel music always permeating Labelle's vocal blend, even more so after they broke free from the girl-group restraints of smoothology. For those who've not had the experience, imagine being a child surrounded by a formidable choir belting out a gospel song and how that might feel to ears ripe for love. During several of my teenage years spent in a Cleveland reformatory called Blossom Hill, we wards of the state were given the choice of attending Baptist or Catholic services on Sundays. What a toss-up: Musical intoxication? Or a Mary-had-a-little-lamb plod? Rocking the crucible of gospel on Sunday mornings was our weekly high. I felt that sound in my bones, knew how to roughneck a note into grace. What gospel music evokes in a body and throat comes from the deepest well of generational grief, the notes transforming the past into joy in the communal present. This is the kindred "it" my choirgirl sisters recognized in me.

What I did not share with Blossom Hill's faux-hoodlum choirgirls were the things they carried: the legacy of slavery and racism. I didn't understand my whiteness as protection or privilege because I was a child and had never experienced either. My experience until then was of poverty, of violent trauma and familial abandonment. And when we sang together, I felt us recognizing one another beneath the skin. Had I not perceived the mercy inside that music as our emotional connection, if my Black choir mates had not related to me based on our similarities as opposed to holding up the differences society drilled into us, I wouldn't have survived. The loneliness, and the ugliness, of society's ills would have been too acute to bear.

We never talked much about race, why we were jailed, or what happened inside our families that pushed us into our shared teenage destiny. Not that racial rifts never happened. There were incidents, accidents. Yet when we sang together, the secret personal weights I carried felt lifted, all heaviness evaporating as we girls joined notes in a communal redemption. Gospel music can cook suffering into a liberating brew of deep sustenance, and no matter the trauma you bury and carry, "There Is a Balm in Gilead" is a prescriptive for heartache. Hearing the voices of Labelle brought me home to the sound that loved me up in my childhood. Every triad of notes, every harmony in the Labellian chain has, at its root, the healing blessedness of gospel music. A gospel choir is an assassin of loneliness. From girl to girl the notes pass in a roundelay, exemplified in a song Nona would write for Labelle one day called "I Believe That I've Finally Made It Home."

— 2 —

REGARDING "MR. LEE"

In the sixties, God was a young black girl
who could sing.

GERRY GOFFIN, quoted by Kathleen Thompson

Decades before riot grrrls and the fierce women singer-songwriters of the 1980s and early '90s, before women in punk and no wave, before the "women's music" of second-wave feminism and the electrifying voices of women in rap and hip-hop, a "girls to the front" musical tidal wave rolled over America. The girl-group genre and its phenomenon in musical history is a crucial setting for Labelle's origin story. There were at least five thousand records released between 1956 and 1967 featuring girl-group voices passionately narrating stories of teen love.[1] With few exceptions, the women riding this first wave were, as Nina Simone intoned in 1969, young, gifted, and Black. The girl-group genre marked an exceptional moment in American history when Black women ascended en masse to the zenith of popular culture.

Patti LaBelle and the Bluebelles were among that wave,

charting Top 40 pop with "I Sold My Heart to the Junkman" (their biggest girl-group hit, peaking at number fifteen pop), "Down the Aisle (The Wedding Song)," and "You'll Never Walk Alone." They might not have had the same level of commercial success as other girl groups—for instance, rivals the Supremes—yet Patti LaBelle and the Bluebelles stood out from the pack, were beyond compare when it came to Patti's vocal pyrotechnics and their exceptional vocal blend. Talent aside, they faced formidable competition from girl groups supported by the star-making machinery of Motown, Phil Spector, and Shadow Morton.

Early girl-group hits included the Bobbettes' "Mr. Lee," the Chantels' scorcher "Maybe," and the gorgeous Weil-Mann composition "Uptown," performed by the Crystals. The Shirelles (a favorite group of Patti, Nona, and Sarah's) had hit after hit, making it to number one in 1960 with the Carole King/Gerry Goffin–penned "Will You Love Me Tomorrow." In the late 1950s, teenage girls were falling in love to the swoony boysong of doo-wop, but when they began to hear themselves on the radio, it was revelatory. Forming groups all over the country and singing their hearts out in basements and bedrooms, musicking girls seized the joy of girl-gang companionship and performance, and, sometimes, the validation a hit record can bring. A hit song could catapult singers from having zero social power to being queens of the neighborhood *and* the airwaves. Because the naïve lyrical themes of the songs are all about love and courtship, people underestimate the impact of this genre. In fact, it was the first female musical revolution, with scores of young women seizing agency and empowerment through the vehicle of song.

Black doo-woppers, girl groups, and the entertainers of Motown and Stax all presented a high-glamour image of sophistication and polish. Along with romantic lyrical themes and brilliant musical arrangements, this was a Black identity white folks felt comfortable with. In conversation with Berry Gordy about Motown, Martin Luther King Jr. called the phenomenon an "emotional integration."[2] Girl-group music was oxytocin for young hearts, potions to fall heter-over-heels in love to. Initially, the sound was an amalgam of stride piano, doo-wop, and rhythm and blues, featuring a passionate lead vocal supported by gospel and doo-wop-inspired backing harmonies. The vested interests of society as dictated by music managers and record company groomers made sure performers toed the line in lyrics and costume. Strictly gendered uniforms were mandatory. This was the heteronormative binary in full bloom, the singers' physical presentation mirroring the dominant white culture of the 1950s and early '60s: *The Donna Reed Show*, *The Mickey Mouse Club*, and Ozzie and Harriet.

Black girl groups wore straight-haired wigs with Jackie Kennedy flips (see the Bluebelles working their flips on the cover of the 45 rpm "Down the Aisle"). The young Bobbettes appear on the sleeve of "Mr. Lee" wearing white, ultrafeminine puff-sleeved dresses, faces framed by wide Peter Pan collars and marcelled hair. In the 1950s, if Black entertainers wanted to make it in America, they dressed to assimilate, to never signal complaint, in exchange for a ticket from racism's subjugation to national admiration. Black truths were not revealed in doo-wop or girl-group music, although they were sometimes strongly hinted; for example, in the masquerade of "The Great Pretender" by the Platters: "Too real is this feeling of make-believe, too real when I feel what my heart can't conceal."

The escaped slave, abolitionist, and women's rights activist Sojourner Truth sold her memoirs and a photograph of herself on cartes de visite with this caption: "I sell the shadow to support the substance."[3] Truth owned the copyright to her own image, the "shadow" of which she speaks, commenting that she "used to be sold for other people's benefit, but now she sold herself for her own." This would also be true for Labelle when they became businesswomen in the early 1970s, finally in control of their own image, songs, and publishing; just as rare for women in music then as was Truth's copyright in 1864. When they began their musical journey, this costumed shadow was fundamental to the sell in segregated America.

Girl-group lyrical concerns were about winning a guy, losing a guy, praying for or competing with another girl over a guy (no matter how lousy of a jerk he might be), inciting people to dance, or bemoaning a motorcycle rebel boy's fatal crash. Female audiences couldn't seem to get enough of wedding songs, and the girl groups pumped them out aplenty: the Dixie Cups' "Chapel of Love," the

Deltairs' "Standing at the Altar," the Hearts' "Disappointed Bride," and on, and on. In fact, the second Top 40 hit by Patti LaBelle and the Bluebelles was "Down the Aisle (The Wedding Song)." Musical accompaniment on these records was initially spare, with garage-band edges, reverb, and echo effects gracing vocal blends and instrumentation with a haunting sonic glamour. "Church" is one among many settings on the reverb units used in recording studios, mimicking the acoustic glory of sacred architecture, a hearkening back to the gospel sound at the root of girl-group harmony.

On the grandest of productions by audio storytellers Shadow Morton and Phil Spector, reverb is piled on thick enough to create a spectral resonance that'll drop you into the presence of your personal idea of holiness. Sound effects—ocean waves, seagulls, motorcycles, thunderstorms—punch the melodrama, inviting you inside these aural movies. Extreme examples are Morton's melodramatic production of the Shangri-Las' "Leader of the Pack" and Spector's "Walking in the Rain" by the Ronettes—pop records frosted with vocal marzipan. Feast on a dozen girl-group songs and you might OD on all that insulin.

The girl groups were a radical sonic departure from the female vocal harmony groups preceding them in the 1950s and late 1940s. White groups like the Fontane Sisters, the McGuire Sisters, and the Chordettes were as smooth and dry as sauvignon blanc, minus the buzz. You can practically feel Lawrence Welk's bubble machine struggling to add some enchantment to their "Donna Reed meets Stepford wife" conformity. Surprising, since the popular female vocal groups of the preceding war years knew a thing or two about rhythm. Acrobats of swing like New Orleans's Boswell Sisters swooped notes wild and tight, delivering close jazzy harmonies while octave hopping over tempos within songs. The Boswells created homophonic vocal displays far more sophisticated than the Andrews, who are better known. And what about the Pope Sisters? Bookended in time by the sisters Boswell and Andrews, a quartet of young, glamorous Black women were wowing audiences in Mobile, Alabama, and in nightclubs all along the Atlantic Coast. With their super tight harmonies, scat style, and staccato rhythms, the Pope Sisters were clearly a musical phenomenon, but like neutrinos, they've slipped through the universe undetected. The only existing Pope Sisters performance I found was a clip on YouTube from a film by pioneering director Oscar Micheaux.[4]

Members of the girl groups were often treated like so many pieces on a music industry chessboard—interchangeable per the whims of male producers, managers, and record company executives. In the film *20 Feet from Stardom*, Darlene Love narrates an egregious tale of thievery. Darlene was the lead singer of the Blossoms, providing the lead vocal on the Phil Spector–produced "He's a Rebel," but the Blossoms were never credited. They were touring at the time, and Spector wanted to rush the record out and start promoting. He credited a different group available to do the live promo dates, the Crystals, robbing Love and her Blossom sisters of credit. "He's a Rebel" became a smash hit and remains a classic of the genre, overwhelmingly due to Darlene Love's lead vocal. The same thing happened to the Starlets, original singers on "I Sold My Heart to the Junkman," which became the Bluebelles' first hit. Harold Robinson did replace the Starlets' vocals with Patti and the Bluebelles, but not until the Starlets filed a lawsuit.

The majority of hit girl-group songs were fabricated on the assembly lines of Motown and the Brill Building by the premier pop songwriting teams of the era. The Funk Brothers for Motown and the Los Angeles–based Wrecking Crew were the session musicians on most tracks, the latter crew responsible for cocreating Phil Spector's Wall of Sound. I was surprised to discover that several of the first girl groups to chart actually wrote their own songs. In 1957, the quirky "Mr. Lee" was penned by the Bobbettes as a put-down of the "ugliest" high school teacher they'd ever seen. Bosses at Atlantic Records made them switch the message from a diss to a crush. Mr. Lee became the "handsomest" teacher, and the song charted Top 10, selling millions of discs. The Chantels soon followed the Bobbettes' success with a hit written by lead singer Arlene Smith: the dramatic, heartrending "Maybe." (Smith's songwriting credit has vanished on several label iterations.)

Regarding "Mr. Lee," the phenomenon of girl gangs singing together proved to be far more than a gimmick; these records made the clouds open and pour coin as the hits came fast and furious. The most lucrative revenues in recorded music are generated from songwriting and publishing royalties. Thankfully, the Bobbettes are credited as songwriters on "Mr. Lee" but not as publishers. I'll take a wild guess that due to this surprise hit, money monsters swooped in, lassoing the royalties by transferring songwriting duties to Brill Building writers, producers, managers, and record company owners, who in turn chained the songs to their own publishing companies.

The Bobbettes, the first girl group in the genre to break the Top 10, with "Mr. Lee," must not have been too happy about compromising their feelings on that 1957 hit. They never had a follow-up success. It certainly wouldn't be the "answer song" they wrote and recorded in 1959, a tune called "I Shot Mr. Lee." The record was nixed by Atlantic, so the Bobbettes released it on a different label called Triple-X. Triple-X was sued by Atlantic, and any existing "I Shot Mr. Lee" records were seized and buried.

Girl-group vocalists are often diminished in the story of rock in favor of superstar producers and hit songwriting teams elevated as the genre's creators and champions. The singers were considered featherweights on the music biz seesaw, when in fact they were the blue-collar workers of audio magick, the voices a nation danced and swooned to. Some call the 1960s (after '64) the golden age of civil rights, in part due to Black music's ascendance on the radio, music beloved and celebrated by all. The truth beneath was *not* broadcast: that on the ground, for Black musicians traveling the Chitlin' Circuit in support of the music, Jim Crow's wingspan was as wide and as threatening as ever. Young women defying danger to entertain and lift spirits, the girl groups were freedom riders, whether they were conscious of it or not.

The Bluebelles endured intense racism on the road. They toured endlessly, laying out their emotions in recording booths and on stages, doing the grueling work of promotion long after the song-meisters left the studio for another girl group, another recording. Performance royalty theft (royalties for the physical performance of the singers on wax) was endemic. Most groups were given just enough (*Isn't fame enough, girls?*) to keep them happy, healthy, and working, a rule that also applied to the Bluebelles. If a bolder singer spoke up or out of turn, she was easily replaced. Yet if not for the singers, all the ink-drenched record moguls, superstar songwriters, and producers would be nameless today. Royalty swindling was an equal-opportunity thief, color and gender blind. Take Frankie Lymon. Manipulated away from his backup friends the Teenagers and robbed of royalties, the isolation helped push him into heroin addiction and early death. Tough girls the Shangri-Las sold millions of records but were robbed of performance royalties. The songwriting Shirelles ended up in a lawsuit with Florence Greenberg, owner and founder of Scepter Records. Greenberg was the sole woman to capitalize on the girl-group sound by owning a string of record labels, proving that women could be just as criminal as the "hit" men.

From the point of view of the girls, though, better to be a pawn onstage at *American Bandstand*, broadcast into millions of living rooms, than to not be in play at all.

Sarah Dash spoke to me about royalties, or lack of, for the Bluebelles during this period:

> At the time, we were not all that astute when it came to business. We were teenagers. We left our homes and we went on the road. We had no knowledge of royalties, no knowledge really of the business. What we knew is that we loved to sing, and we loved to be onstage. We had the ability to blend and bring happiness to people. I'm not sure if they stole . . . or, I would say, we didn't get any [royalties] from that time. We did at one point receive an advance [from Harold Robinson], but it wasn't all that.

I imagine how the Bluebelles must have felt during the relentless road tours of the 1960s. To sing, to hear the applause and know you're genuinely bringing it, creating so much excitement in the audience that it turns circular; the giving and taking in a communal moment of music, well, it's an ecstatic way to live. Trouble is, for all those years of hellacious road travel and so many hundreds of shows and records sold, the pennies never did add up. Singing and performing is serious *work*. Rehearsing day and night—not just the harmonies and arrangements but the charm-school choreography. Oh, and they may be cute, but T-strap heels are hell on the feet, especially when you're fending off sexual assaults. *Working your last nerve.* Trying to find lodging, a decent meal, a clean bathroom while driving through the racist South. And masquerading a white-sanctified version of woman equals hours of beauty prep. We're talking high-femme-drag-requiring effort, time, and a repetitive cycle of nightly sweat. *Work those lashes!* Micromanaged. Pimped when it came to royalties. But then, the climax. The stage, and the audience love. Making it all worth it.

Nona, Patti, Sarah, and Cindy shared the same highs, challenges, and injustices as most of the genre's groups and singers. The presentation of romantic naïveté, nonthreatening emotions, and the performance of passivity (in gender and pocket) continued for the girl groups until the early 1970s. Until the bravest among them turned soul-rebel wild.

— 3 —

SWEETHEARTS OF THE APOLLO

Car salesman turned record label owner Harold B. Robinson kept the Bluebelles under contract for eight singles. Where their first hit, "I Sold My Heart to the Junkman," has that "take the playground to church" sound of the early girl groups, "Down the Aisle (The Wedding Song)" sounds closest to straight-up doo-wop. The latter charted Top 40 pop, but Robinson's finances tanked just as demand for the Bluebelles' live performances took on steam. They were gigging more than 320 days out of the year, mostly one-nighters, the highs of show biz tainted by the excruciating rigors of traveling the circuit crammed into a hooptie of a station wagon. Robinson cut his losses by selling "Down the Aisle" to King Records. Bernard Montague remained as manager, and a record company shuffle ensued. The Bluebelles signed with Cameo-Parkway Records, moved to Nicetown Records, and then moved to Newtime Records, with release dates and labels ajumble through several years of recordings. "You'll Never Walk Alone" seems to have been issued on at least four labels in the space of two years. (A common tactic used to pocket artists' royalties: label owners shift recordings to different companies in a game of Russian dolls, knowing the artists can't afford forensic audits. The practice continues today.)

While indie record sharks played a shell game with their records, the Bluebelles were one of, if not *the*, hardest-working girl-group acts of the 1960s. Patti sounds teen-age remarkable on these records, that voice, rocking the grooves in part due to the cradle of Bluebelle harmonies. In 1964, three Bluebelles turned twenty (they called Cindy, who is a bit older, "Mom"). With the support of Nona, Sarah, and Cindy, Patti does Rodgers and Hammerstein's "You'll Never Walk Alone" no less justice than Mahalia Jackson, Frank Sinatra, Judy Garland, and Aretha Franklin. "Down the Aisle" was another lyrical bid for a place in the hetero hegemony, but the song's languid tempo and its lack of a catchy chorus kept it from climbing to the top of the charts.

Teenage girls adore singing along to their favorite hits, but Patti's brand of vocal arson often prohibits sing-alongs, rendering many of the Bluebelles' early recordings a spectator sport, unless the listeners are singing the backing vocals. The Bluebelles were still several years away from the unfettered roar of choruses you can't help but sing along to in their Labelle incarnation. The spooky reverb that can lift a slow song into the spectral is also missing from these early records. Too many strikes and you're out—of Top 20 radio chart success.

Live and direct was another story. The toughness of

the crowd at Harlem's Apollo Theater is legend, a legacy continuing today, with 1,600 seats able to make or break an entertainer. From the Bluebelles' first performances in 1962, the theater's embrace earned them the moniker "Sweethearts of the Apollo." No other girl group on the Apollo bill dared follow the Bluebelles, especially after Patti let loose on the closing song of their set, "You'll Never Walk Alone," resolving the song on a high C7 note. These performances often sent the Harlem audience into collective seizure. Among the converts was a young Luther Vandross. Hooked on the Bluebelles' records and their shows at the Apollo, Luther cocreated their first fan club. He was so enamored that he snuck backstage once carrying a few gowns, pretending he was a designer so he could meet his heroines. Speaking about the group and the later incarnation we would know from *Nightbirds*, Luther testified, "They were the best group sound, the best blend I'd ever heard."[1]

Nona tells a story about the Apollo:

It was 1961 or '62. I don't know the exact date, but I remember what we wore and what we performed. . . . We walked onstage after Brook Benton, and the headliner was Dinah Washington. And I think the Drifters were on that show. By the end of that show, I was like, "Oh my God, this is real." We were wearing sailor outfits and singing "I Sold My Heart to the Junkman" and "Danny Boy" and "Down the Aisle." We did kill it. . . . The defining moment was when the drag queens and the boxers at the Saturday night late show stood up and applauded.[2]

The Bluebelles were a live sensation with a stellar rep, but by 1965 they found themselves without a record label. They continued to hit the road as the geography of the music business shifted, its compass magnetized by the new sounds coming out of Britain.

Despite their lack of Top 20 pop hits, the tight musical nature of the Bluebelles supporting Patti's vocal agility positioned Patti as the "leader of the pack" of girl-group vocalists. Enthusiastic word of mouth about the group's thrilling performances traveled across the pond, catching the attention of the Rolling Stones, five London boys slavishly in love with the sound of Black America. With their badass attitudes and appreciation of American blues, I bet they heard "Junkman" and shared a smirk, attributing it, as I once did, to another kind of junk. The Stones invited Patti and the Bluebelles to open their American tour in 1965. We're talking early quintessential Stones here, at their rock and roll hottest and rowdiest; the boys Simon Napier-Bell said looked like "rough trade from the meat-rack behind Piccadilly Circus."[3] The tour was in support of the LP *Out of Our Heads*. Coming off of hits that included "(I Can't Get No) Satisfaction," the Stones painted it Black for the tour, covering Marvin Gaye's "Hitch Hike," Don Covay's "Mercy, Mercy," and Otis Redding's "That's How Strong My Love Is."

Touring with the early Stones? On their private plane? Despite the hallway monitoring of chaperone Bernard Montague, with his curfews, rules, and fines, imagine the education gleaned from the Glimmer Twins plus Brian Jones, Charlie, Bill, and entourage. In an interview with Britain's *Express*, Vicki recounts how Andrew Loog Oldham, the Stones' manager, carried around "a lovely box of wonderfully coloured ups and downs that looked like Smarties."[4] The backstage shenanigans coupled with the onstage strut of the Stones must have been an eye-opener; a rock and roll high school immersion for three rock stars in waiting.

In her memoir, Patti tells of how the racism of the South shocked and upset the bad-boy rockers. Because the Bluebelles were banned from staying in many of the same hotels as the Stones, in Patti's estimation their destruction of hotel rooms could be read as an "f-you" to American racism. Imagine if the Bluebelles, the ones on the receiving end of the racism, had performed the same stunts in protest.

Due in part to the cachet of having toured with the Stones and of contributing to the Atlantic compilation LP *Saturday Night at the Uptown*, Patti LaBelle and the Bluebelles signed to Atlantic Records in 1965. They recorded more than thirty tracks for the label over four years, the highest charter being a cover of "Over the Rainbow," a song Patti absolutely blazes on. The Atlantic recordings are a farrago of production styles, culminating in doom for any band or artist who doesn't fit into a well-defined genre.

My favorite 45 from the Atlantic years is "I'm Still Waiting," written and produced by Curtis Mayfield. On it you hear the signature string arrangements unique to Mayfield, his signature sensuality of melodic drama apparent in his recordings with the Impressions. Mayfield's style eventually culminated in his soundtrack for *Superfly* and the lushness of a song like "Give Me Your Love." His arrangement for "I'm Still Waiting" is a well-suited wrap around Patti's dramatic delivery and the Bluebelles' accompanying vocal web. A gorgeous production and arrangement, the song would climb into the low thirties on the R&B singles chart, then disappear. Of all the producers and writers the early Bluebelles worked with, Curtis Mayfield, musical genius and visionary, stands apart from the rest. If Mayfield had produced an entire LP of songs for them, what an extraordinary record they would have made together.

"I'm Still Waiting" did not happen for the Bluebelles, and Mayfield rerecorded the song with the Impressions in 1967. Despite the record's lukewarm reception, the Bluebelles' meeting with Mayfield was fortunate, as he went on to encourage Nona to write songs. She brought her first song to Mayfield, "I Need Your Love," cowritten with the Bluebelles. The song was recorded as a B side for one of many Atlantic singles and went unnoticed, but Mayfield's support was a booster shot to a fledgling writer's confidence.

Why didn't Patti LaBelle and the Bluebelles become a household name in the 1960s, like the Shirelles, the

Shangri-Las, the Supremes, the Marvelettes, or Martha Reeves and the Vandellas? The latter three acts had the power of Berry Gordy's Motown factory in Detroit, staffed by songwriters and producers such as Holland-Dozier-Holland, Marvin Gaye, and Smokey Robinson, and musicians the Funk Brothers. The Shirelles, the Chiffons, and the Crystals had Brill Building songwriters Carole King and Gerry Goffin, Cynthia Weil and Barry Mann, and the Shangri-Las had Shadow Morton, Jeff Barry, and Ellie Greenwich, as well as musicians the Wrecking Crew. These teams were superstar hit machines. They churned out fantastic pop songs for the girl groups, often tailoring lead melodies as exclusive fits for individual lead singers.

What support did the Bluebelles have, aside from their loyal audience? A car salesman (not to disparage Robinson, who was responsible for launching their career) and a somewhat green husband-and-wife management team with minimal connections. The days of their beloved Mo Bailey drilling them on syncopated steps were long gone; there was no Cholly Atkins (choreographer for Motown) behind the scenes, no Motown artist development classes or superstar studio bands. This girl group was DIY all the way.

Watching old clips of the Bluebelles, it's apparent that Patti can sing Saturnian rings around Diana Ross. But given that the group were recording covers of "Over the Rainbow" and "Danny Boy" for Atlantic, one has to ask, were the Bluebelles auditioning for a spot in Vegas at the Sands Hotel? After touring with the Rolling Stones?

What made Martha and the Vandellas memorable? A song called "Dancing in the Street," written by Marvin Gaye, Mickey Stevenson, and Ivy Jo Hunter, recorded at Hitsville USA. The Vandellas and that song were nurtured in the warm embrace of Motown, shot from the Hitsville cannon straight to the top of the charts. A cover of the mournful Irish ballad "Danny Boy" was not about to do the same for Patti LaBelle and the Bluebelles.

By the end of the 1960s, the British invasion had upended the game, with self-contained male groups writing and performing their own songs to young women who couldn't get enough of feminized bad boys and their musical swagger. Stateside, chart toppers like Aretha Franklin's "Respect" and "Think" and Nancy Sinatra's "These Boots Are Made for Walkin'" were proving pop music was no longer the sole province of dreamy submissive females beholden to the whims of their men.

So what came next for this girl group with the octave-leaping vocalist? They continued to build a loyal audience, tour by grueling tour, and to rock the Apollo whenever the chance arrived. They kept at it in the studio, and a few gems emerged; "All or Nothing" was recorded in 1966,[5] produced by Bert Berns, the American writer, producer, and pond-hopper behind the Beatles' smash hit "Twist and Shout." The recording has the dramatic arrangements in step with the time (as in Phil Spector and Shadow Morton), and the group's performance is stellar, but again the record was neglected by Atlantic. They also recorded "Take Me for a Little While," a song waiting for the right voices and production to make it a hit, first covered in 1965 by the dark-throated singer Evie Sands (she's been lost to history for the most part). The song would be endlessly covered, but it was Dusty Springfield who sang all hell out of it on her 1967 LP *Where Am I Going?*

"Where am I going?" became a more suitable refrain for the Bluebelles in 1967, when the earth shifted on its axis: Cindy Birdsong disappeared. She simply vanished without a word to her bandmates, leaving the three singers bewildered. Soon enough, the Bluebelles discovered their nemesis Diana Ross had poached Cindy for the Supremes, as replacement for Florence Ballard. It couldn't have happened at a more vulnerable moment for the Bluebelles. In nearly every interview in which Patti is asked about Cindy Birdsong's departure, as well as in her memoir, she tells of how the betrayal devastated the group. All three singers speak of Cindy's departure as a major heartbreak. It would ultimately pull Nona, Patti, and Sarah tighter together.

The Supremes were still going strong in 1968, releasing "Love Child," a departure from the usual girl-group themes of loving, losing, and longing. The record hit number one and stayed there for two weeks, introducing a new narrative to pop with a story about an illegitimate Black girl growing up in poverty. This success must have felt baneful to the Bluebelles, especially in light of Cindy's treason. By 1969 Diana Ross would ascend to Supreme Being, with her group an adjunct to her name. A year later, Patti LaBelle and the Bluebelles flipped the name switch and, as Labelle, eventually eclipsed Diana Ross and the Supremes as a creative force imperial.

The trio recorded several more songs for Atlantic, but none of them charted high enough to please the hit men. William Morris and Dinah Washington's agency, Queen Booking, kept them in gigs, but for all the rough times on the road, they barely made ends meet. They recorded "Oh My Love," their first single without Cindy. Patti fills up 90 percent of the vocal space, yet despite her stellar delivery, the record didn't perform well. A few lukewarm releases later, Ahmet Ertegun and the Atlantic team hit an impasse with the Bluebelles. Atlantic sent them to London in a last-ditch effort of support. They would perform on the groundbreaking *Ready Steay Go!* (*RSG!*) television show. *RSG!* altered popular music forever by introducing rock and soul to Great Britain. Patti and the Bluebelles' London appearance resulted in a fated meeting with *RSG!*'s groovy young female producer. She wore the latest Carnaby Street fashions, topped by a shaggy blonde haircut à la Jane Fonda in *Klute* before the barber known for creating the iconic cut put scissors to the shape. She moonlighted as a rock journalist while trolling the clubs in Soho, looking for new talent to book on the show. Enamored with the Bluebelles' act, she booked them for two weeks straight, and a friendship was born. The producer's name was Vicki Wickham.

When the Bluebelles returned to the States, their management contract with Bernard Montague ended; he'd signed the Delfonics, choosing not to remain with the Blue-belles. The Atlantic record deal expired without a pickup. The Bluebelles continued touring, but the money was so meager, they could barely scrape by from gig to gig. Girl groups were falling off the charts. Solo female singers with top hits in '69 were the consistently charting divas Are-tha, Dionne Warwick, and Dusty Springfield. Radio DJs were feeling the heat of social unrest and were playing what they liked, what needed to be heard as opposed to the songs accompanied by the heaviest payola. And there was so much to like.

Although chart success and a decent payday proved elu-sive, the Bluebelles stayed together. Patti could have easily gone solo, especially in light of Cindy's exodus and the dis-appointment the group suffered during the Atlantic years. The end of the Atlantic deal in 1969 would have been the moment to give up, for each to go her own way and pursue solo careers, or sing backing vocals for major artists. Or join a more successful group, as did Cindy. The mark of any great artist is conviction: to the notes, the paint stroke, the words on a page. In the case of Patti, Nona, and Sarah, the conviction was to their bond; as friends, as family, and as a musical force. Several times in her memoir, Patti talks about Nona and Sarah; how she never felt closer to any-one in her life.

Sly and the Family Stone had three Top 10 hits in '69, opening up new possibilities for music and social commen-tary. The album *Stand!* laid it out in the title song, with

Sly singing "It's the truth that the truth makes them so uptight," and "Don't call me nigger, whitey." Roberta Flack released *First Take* and the hit single "The First Time Ever I Saw Your Face," while those of us purchasing the LP were treated to Flack's version of the Gene McDaniels–penned "Compared to What." Nina Simone released "To Be Young, Gifted and Black," dedicating it to her departed friend, playwright Lorraine Hansberry. James Brown's "Say It Loud—I'm Black and I'm Proud" introduced the slapback of *Fuck assimilation, it's time to sing truth to power and dance while we do it!* Socially conscious soul and psychedelia scorched radio waves and dance floors; Jimi Hendrix, Jefferson Airplane, Janis Joplin, and Sly and the Family Stone wailed next to one another on the pop charts. Nineteen sixty-nine was the year of the Stonewall riot and Woodstock, the Manson murders and Altamont, Angela Davis and the Chicago Seven. The energy of rebellion was volatile and unpredictable; a world on fire liable to go either way, reborn from the flames or damned to an eternal beatdown. It was the music holding out hope, inciting change; we all sang along, adding our collective voice to the soundtrack of an American revolution.

How would the Bluebelles fit into the new musical zeitgeist? T-strap shoes kicking a choreographed sway to "Over the Rainbow" were not about to move their years of work toward its next manifestation. A serious recalibration was in order. They'd hooked up with a manager who promised the world but proved to be nearly lethal in his approach.[6] They needed help, were desperate to extricate from a bad situation. Sarah remembered the producer of *Ready Steady Go!*—she'd asked the singers to keep in touch. With Nona and Patti in agreement, Sarah put in a call to London—to Vicki Wickham.

— 4 —

READY STEADY GO!

In a 1975 interview, Labelle spoke of gender discrimination in the music business, with Vicki Wickham watching from the sidelines:

> PATTI: Vicki Wickham is our manager . . . she's not really a manager, because managers don't usually work that way. She's a friend. She's the fourth member of Labelle . . .
>
> SARAH: . . . and our organization, I think it's probably one of the few organizations run by women. We have a woman manager, lawyer, and we're businesswomen . . . now . . .
>
> NONA: . . . thanks to Vicki. In the record industry, you automatically relate it to males because it's male-oriented. When a woman walks into an office and says, "I have an act, I'm their manager," they either go, "Oh wow, what boobs . . . how quick can I 'do' so-and-so?" Or they don't want to know about you because they figure they . . . *can't*. It was hard for us to get across because of that. I'm not saying all of you gentlemen discriminated against us,

but there was some discrimination. And I didn't particu-
larly like it . . .

SARAH: . . . read, baby! (*finger-snaps*)[1]

Endless ink has been spilled on the British Invasion
(including some in this book), its boy bands laying waste
to the popularity of the girl groups while panicking Brill
Building songwriters. We hear much less about the American soul invasion of buttoned-up post–World War II Britain, or that it was two women, Vicki Wickham and Dusty
Springfield, who introduced soul music to England through
British television.

In January of 1966, the Bluebelles performed the Bert
Berns–produced track "All or Nothing" on *RSG!* It's the
track I feel sounds closest to the dramatic arrangements
heard from groups like the Ronettes and the Shangri-Las,
yet the record was underpromoted by Atlantic, who clearly
didn't understand how to promote the group. Vicki had
an eye for talent (she booked an unknown Jimi Hendrix
on *RSG!*) and immediately saw the Bluebelles' potential.
She approached Atlantic's copresident Jerry Wexler about
producing a few songs for the group, but this was the 1960s
(not that much has changed), and Wexler wasn't about to
put a woman in the producer's seat. He underestimated Ms.
Vicki Heather Wickham OBE (Officer of the Most Excel-
lent Order of the British Empire), *and* the three women
soon to be known as Labelle.

Vicki Wickham was born in Newbury, Berkshire, on a

farm west of London. Newbury was bombed by the Nazis in 1943. In the dead of winter, she recalls, there were no warning sirens, just the sudden sound of explosions. She was four years old at the time and remembers crawling into a cupboard with her mum, huddling beneath shelves loaded with glass jars used for preserving jam. A detonation nearly rocked the house off its foundation. Vicki remembers the sound of Mason jars rattling around them but does not remember fear. The farmer's daughter grew up to become a trailblazing visionary, remaining fearless throughout her extraordinary career. She arrived in London at sixteen, determined to find a job in a creative field—in 1950s England, nigh impossible for a young woman. (World War II was over, and the soldiers it did not ruin returned to Britain, to jobs temporarily filled by women.) On the Nona-penned song "Phoenix," released in 1975, Patti sings, "Hiding thoughts of new ways in old Mason jars," a reference to their visionary manager's childhood experience.

Postwar London's stylish youth culture was clever, classless (or imagined itself to be), and free, as in *the kids are alright* (a nod to the boys who'd represent all that was quintessentially mod, the Who). Vicki was drawn to Wardour Street and its clubs: the Flamingo, the Scene, and the Marquee. The music show *Ready Steady Go!* was fulcrum to everything swinging about 1960s London. Vicki started work at *RSG!* as a secretary but quickly became an integral part of the production team. She had such good instincts for where youth culture was pointing and what it valued that *RSG!* coproducer Francis Hitching described her as a "conscience for the pop world."[2]

Broadcast on Friday nights on ITV, *Ready Steady Go!* was an immediate sensation, exploding into England's sitting rooms in the summer of 1963 with the slogan "The weekend starts here!" Teens went bananas for the show, while adults were alternately bewildered, mesmerized, and somewhat horrified, watching their teenagers shake off the stuffiness of postwar Britain while dancing the Hully Gully and the Cavern Stomp to the Beatles, barefooted Sandie Shaw, the Who, Cilla Black, and the Rolling Stones. The show's small studio necessitated a vérité style to match the rough-and-ready sounds of the new music, and between the band members, their instruments and gear, audience, and crew, the monolithic rolling camera rigs had no room to shoot around each other and nearly mowed down the dancers. We see it all in the frame—cameras, cables, lights, teacups—the lack of polish and gritty authenticity making it feel like a punk show in vitro. Having a ticket for *RSG!* as an audience member or a dancer served as catapult to hip social status; you might get to hang out with Lulu, the Animals, or Mick, Keef, and Brian. And in the center of the action stood Vicki Wickham, waving her conductor's wand.

Dusty Springfield fell in love with American soul music while touring stateside in the early 1960s. Performing on *Ready Steady Go!*, she became fast friends with Wickham. Together these white, queer, trailblazing women plotted the soul invasion of the British Isles, coproducing the *RSG!* special edition entitled "The Sounds of Motown" in March of 1965. Choppy pieces of the show appear on YouTube in a confusing jumble, but one highlight I discovered (thanks to Gayle Wald) was presenter Dusty and performer Martha Reeves entering the studio set from opposite sides, meeting in the middle of the stage to sing "Wishin' and Hopin'," the Bacharach-David tune. Dusty included herself as both a presenter and the sole white singer in this special. It's a fantastic moment; Martha and Dusty camp it up on the song, making fun of their own high-femme realness. They point at one another's wigs and giggle knowingly about the masquerade.

Gayle Wald writes about performers Martha and the Vandellas and Sister Rosetta Tharpe arriving in England in 1964, as well as the *RSG!* special, soon to be followed by Berry Gordy's distribution deal with EMI UK and an influx of soul music to the British Isles. She critiques the performance of Dusty with Martha and the Vandellas: "I want to loosely and somewhat promiscuously name this intimacy 'girl group transnationalism'—a term that would include various modes of gendered sociality, including female friendships, homosocial flirtations, and forms of musical sisterhood or brotherhood based on shared aesthetics and progressive, anti-racist politics—and suggest that it has a place in our narratives of the Black Atlantic music of the 1960s."[3]

The camerawork on the "Sounds of Motown" special presented standard wide performance shots and introduced

B-cameras punching into the wide shots for extreme close-ups on the super-emotive entertainers: the Temptations, Marvin Gaye, Martha and the Vandellas, and others. A significant moment occurs when the Supremes perform "Stop! In the Name of Love." The online editor switches to a super close shot on Diana Ross's face, her shiny lipstick glittering in the stage lights. Refusing to ignore Florence Ballard and Mary Wilson, the girls are graced with the close-ups they too deserve. The British audiences tuning in to the show experienced intimate close-ups of Black faces for the first time, presenting the undeniable beauty of soul expression through song. In a Marshall McLuhan instance of the medium being the message, Diana's arm extends in the traffic cop halt gesture, an extreme close-up on her hand filling the frame on "STOP!," her hand then flipping upside down on the beat into a finger-snap. The camera refocuses to the two singers behind Diana as her hand pulls out of frame. *Stop in the name of love* indeed: a loaded image entering the sitting rooms of Britain, heralding an anti-apartheid musical era. (Speaking of apartheid, trailblazer Dusty toured South Africa in 1964, where she insisted on performing an unscheduled show for an integrated audience. The South African government quickly terminated the tour and deported her.)

While the Motown *RSG!* show rocked a revolution in Britain, Patti and the Bluebelles went home to continue working for hits with Atlantic. Their cover of the Brit pop song "Groovy Kind of Love" was released in the same window as vanilla rockers the Mindbenders' original version (the latter shot to number two on the pop charts), and although Patti's performance on the *Wizard of Oz* classic "Over the Rainbow" was astonishing, hits continued to remain elusive. Throughout the mid- to late sixties, the Bluebelles kept touring and recording, their song choices and lingering girl-group mannerisms clearly out of step with the times.

Peek under the lid of any style revolution and there's a good chance you'll find a party of gay men and women plotting a cultural coup d'état. *RSG!* was no exception, and the story of Labelle includes a cavalcade of queerdom where many roads lead back to soul chanteuse Dusty Springfield. In 1966, Dusty was moved to tears by a dramatic Italian love song called "Io che non vivo (senza te)." She was desperate for an English version of the lyrics. Vicki Wickham cowrote the new lyrics with her gay friend Simon Napier-Bell; he managed the Yardbirds and Marc Bolan and later managed George Michael's Wham!. Vicki and Simon finished the chorus in a taxicab on their way to a club, and Dusty's Italian song, now called "You Don't Have to Say You Love Me," hit number one in the UK.

Queer circles crossed again when Vicki featured the Who on *RSG!*, becoming fast friends with their management team, Cockney Chris Stamp (brother of Terence) and posh Kit Lambert. The duo's company, Track Records, would become a subsidiary of London Records. Kit and Chris signed the Who to Track Records, as well as the Jimi

Hendrix Experience, and they would sign the newly minted Labelle. (Track Records released Jimi's first single, "Hey Joe," which charted number two in the UK.) Kit Lambert was loaded (as in money, drink, and powder), haute gay, and as archly excessive as he was imaginative. He provoked his lads to flirt with danger. In rock and roll, danger is like whipped cream: you want to bury your face in it. Kit was the guy pushing wild boy Keith Moon to go bat-guano crazy on the drums, also shelling out worthwhile pounds sterling for all those Pete Townshend–smashed Rickenbackers and Strats.

Napier-Bell described gay image makers in the music scene of the 1960s as feeling quite comfortable with irreverence and risk-taking. Another impresario springs to mind: the conservative-appearing Brian Epstein, beloved gay manager of the Beatles. Andrew Loog Oldham flirted with bisexuality and pushed his boys the Rolling Stones toward the scandalous, suggesting they dress in World War II military lady-drag for the artwork on the 1966 single "Have You Seen Your Mother, Baby, Standing in the Shadow?" This rock and roll homo-flirt didn't extend to popular women performers. Yet.

Throughout their artistic journey together, Vicki and Labelle were surrounded by gay male songwriters, designers, record moguls, and friends. All contributed to shaping their story. Reginald Dwight, for example, the piano player in the band Bluesology, backed the Bluebelles and other soul acts like the Isley Brothers when they appeared in England. Nona told me they were great pals with Reggie, and Patti talks about playing the card game tonk with him while touring. LaBelle didn't realize Reggie was Elton John until years later, when he offered the singers tickets to one of his sold-out shows. Lionel Bart, another gay man, was a close friend of Vicki's. Thought of as the "father of the modern British musical," Bart grew up poor in Stepney in London's East End, his childhood informing the work he'd be most known for, the musical *Oliver!*, a show initially rejected by West End producers. *Orphans! Poverty! Who wants to think of such depressing things?* Bart's theatricality and the "panto" shows Wickham loved as a child must have influenced her as she ruminated over the ingredients of rock stardom.

England's gay in-crowd remained locked in the closet, yet it was a decidedly queer brush painting its shimmer over the sexiest of rock's proceedings. Vicki never considered coming out as a lesbian until 1999. Dusty was a bit of an exception. When Dusty declared herself bisexual in an *Evening Standard* article in 1970,[4] there wasn't as much blowback as one would expect, due to her sexuality being an open secret in the sixties. Cavorting celesbians in the 1960s and '70s on both sides of the Atlantic hid their sexuality undercover for fear of ruination. In *Dancing with Demons*,[5] Vicki talks about how Dusty wouldn't have dared come out publicly as a lesbian during the height of her fame (the 1960s), because people would have defined her by her sexuality; never mind that Dusty spent far more earthly hours singing, sleeping, throwing food-laden plates, and drinking than she did sexing. Vicki states in an interview that she "wasn't out in the 60s": "I didn't know what I was, really. Everyone knew I was gay, but we were so un—politically conscious."[6] Exposing one's non-het identity in the 1960s was the equivalent to sticking a toe tag on your career. For all its affectations of the outrageous, rock and roll is still a business, run by men who have always leaned conservative when it comes to the bottom line.

A friendship developed between Vicki and Kit Lambert and Simon Napier-Bell, two gay men responsible for steering the careers of several iconic rock stars. Like her male peers, Vicki knew the elements required to build a rock superstar career: the songs, the fashion and fun, the risk-taking, the erotic edge, the sticking it to the status quo . . . the kids were mad for it all. She booked and debuted the Beatles and the Rolling Stones on *RSG!*, acts that shifted the world of music on its axis. She also wrote for the Brit music rags *Fabulous 208* and *Melody Maker*, penning articles on the Beatles, the Stones, Donny Hathaway, Stevie Wonder, the Mamas and the Papas, Roberta Flack, Yoko Ono, Crosby, Stills, Nash, and Young, and Ashford and Simpson.

When the Bluebelles asked Vicki to manage them in 1969 she was initially unsure; she might have helped launch many a rock star's career through *RSG!*, but she had technically never managed an act. To tip her decision, she invited Kit Lambert and Chris Stamp to the Bluebelles' show at the

Apollo in New York. The Bluebelles were hitting a professional bottom in 1969, but playing the Apollo always guaranteed a home run. The pressure was on that night—and the Bluebelles *killed* under pressure. After experiencing the phenomenon of Patti, Nona, and Sarah onstage, and the fevered passion of their audience, Kit and Chris conspired with Vicki: there was something else going on with the trio, a raw potential of exciting otherness in the vocal pyrotechnics that felt obscured by the traditional songs and outfits. With all that combustion, what might happen if their cocoon of bland were to unravel? I've been in Vicki's company many times. I can hear her mischievous laugh as she tells the power duo, "Leave it to me."

From the moment Vicki and the boys met the Bluebelles after that Apollo show, the party was *on*. It was Vicki's time to put into practice all she'd learned about the making of a rock and roll sensation. Kit opened his checkbook, and the Bluebelles flew to London for a six-month sabbatical with their new manager, Vicki Wickham.

— 5 —

PYROTECHNIC GOSPEL PUNK

The first of seven alchemical steps in the allegorical process of "turning lead into gold" is calcination by fire: a burning away of all excess to reveal a thing's purest essence. In Latin, this essence is called the materia prima. The process can also be described as drilling down to the core realization of the matter at hand; a personal belief, for instance. The twentieth-century alchemist Fulcanelli stated, "All our purifications are done in fire, by fire, and with fire."[1] In late 1969, Patti LaBelle and the Bluebelles found themselves about to face a bonfire of musical and sartorial vanities. Vicki Wickham and a new British record deal brought them 3,500 miles away from their comfort zone, to London, to burn away the masks of propriety and expose the materia prima of their talents.

When Labelle signed with Chris Stamp and Kit Lambert's Track Records, Vicki wanted the trio to break down everything standing between the audience and their wildest essence. I'm talking about the authenticity of imagination that art demands; the inner life unfettered, to dance like beauty with its beast in a new incarnation. Describing their situation in an interview, Vicki recounts, "They were at a low ebb, scraping for gigs. Things had changed, but they hadn't changed, were doing the same material, wearing the same wigs." She recounts pitching to Sarah, Nona, and Patti: "You're three powerful Black women, each with a unique and fantastic voice, and together you're a force of nature. Politics, feminism, eroticism. . . . You're women, and there's a lot to be said."

Patti was the hardest to persuade. "I fought her like a crazy woman," says Patti. "I said, Miss Thing, I'm very, very happy here. I don't want to go to London, I don't want to change our songs, I don't want to change my way of dress, I don't want to change anything."[2]

When Vicki suggested Patti's new look be knickers and knee-high boots, Patti flipped her wig. And she didn't take to the idea of changing the name of the group, was perfectly content with the girl-group naming tradition of Patti and her backing belles. She eventually agreed to folding eight syllables into *one* beauty. From then on, they would be known collectively as Labelle. As for Patti's distaste for knickers and boots? Bottomless.

The changes excited Sarah, and Nona was ready to launch with a notebook full of spark—Vicki encouraged Nona to turn her poems into songs. Patti continued to resist, kicking nearly every idea back to the others. In London, she felt they were ganging up against her at times. It would take some serious calcinating to change her mind. Up until this moment, Patti took up most of the vocal real estate in the trio. Theirs was a blend based on nine years of harmonizing, yet still submerging Nona's and Sarah's voices in obeisance to Patti's lead. This was the typical vocal structure of the majority of girl groups. The structure suited Patti, and despite the Bluebelles' lack of success (in comparison to the superstar Supremes), she was content to bask in the regional spotlight with the support of her two best friends.

Another hindrance: girl-group songs were directed at teenagers, but girl-group lyrical content did not mature with the Bluebelles, or the majority of girl groups. Covering standards wasn't the answer. By the end of the 1960s they were on the verge of becoming an anachronism, sounding more like a vocal ensemble you'd listen to while sipping martinis at the Flamingo. Patti probably thought, *What's wrong with that?* But Vicki had other notions. Rock star ideas. They had amassed a loyal fan base and an entourage of devotees. They were still able to play the circuit, and the success of their live shows did grant a modicum of celebrity to be enjoyed. Big audience love can often make up for a lack of hits, even for meager pay. Patti's attitude was *If it ain't broke, don't try and fix it*, but at some point in the London music rehab, Vicki convinced Patti it wasn't about fixing anything; it was about giving the audience something new, something different. *Solve et coagula* is a Latin expression used in alchemy. It means to break down and then to coagulate the shiny elements into a new and radiant form.

Vicki was well aware that Patti's voice was extraordinary, but she also knew what made the group unique: Nona and Sarah, and the musical sisterhood the three shared. Watching clips of them performing, singing, and interacting, their love for each other as a team comes at you nakedly confident. They'd been through so much together, knew one another inside out. This love, their materia prima, informed the changes as they set to work.

Friend and keyboard player Gene Casey joined them in London. Casey helped lay down the chord structures as the trio commenced writing songs for their first album as Labelle. A note here about songwriting: The general consensus is that any significant contribution to a song's lyric, melody, or structure can be perceived as writing. Nona didn't play an instrument or have much knowledge of music theory back then, but she had imagination and a finely tuned musical instinct. Nona, Patti, or Sarah would sing a melody and lyric to Gene, and he'd strike a few chords on the piano until the group approved the chord structure. The days of tight polite backing vocals framing Patti's voice dissolved as the new material took shape. The three singers began to let it rip together as one, smoothology be damned. Their new sound was more rooted in gospel's furthest sonic frontiers, with a raw, emotional quality, yet weaving harmonically into a gorgeous braid of power.

Long days were filled with scheming, tussling, and singing with Gene, followed by nights of Nona and Sarah hitting London's Soho club scene, sometimes with Vicki, while Patti stayed home to brood. Nona and Sarah were both single, eager to enjoy the excitement of London in 1970. While Patti did her fair share of partying, she was newly married and felt separated, too soon and too long, from her husband. She preferred spending time alone to cope with the changes; the old structure had been broken and there was much to process. Although Patti remained the lead singer, she would own the spotlight no longer, and she was trying to wrap her head around this new vision of the Bluebelles. *Singing rock songs? In black lipstick?* It all felt a bit too wild.

Labelle's debut LP on Track Records/Warner Brothers, simply titled *Labelle*, was produced by Kit Lambert and Vicki Wickham (Lambert was usually MIA, leaving the duties to Vicki). The trio's gospel-baptized voices wailed on a group of cover songs and a few Labelle originals. Nona's and Sarah's voices came loose to play around Patti's, mink-like on a verse, unwrapping with sudden ferocity on a unison chorus. The tracks mix a more contemporary gospel feel with a New Orleans style of R&B and soul-meets-rock guitar licks, while stepping to a more funked-up trajectory of peers Sly and the Family Stone and the Isley Brothers.

The Labelle women loved fashion, including Patti, who eventually warmed up to the London trends. Biba, created by Barbara Hulanicki, was the most fashionable boutique of 1960s London, a favorite of Bowie, Twiggy, Bardot, and the Stones. Sarah recalls, "I wore so much Biba! The black lipstick, the burgundy lipstick. When I came back to Jersey from London, friends and family were like, *Oh my God, look at this woman!* Biba was happening, I loved it." Their debut LP cover introduced the new look for the all-girl band. Replacing the wigs were tight Kathleen Cleaver–style Afros. They pose on gymnasium rings, happily defiant as they funk with gravity; Nona and Sarah hang upside down, signaling future space suspensions, and there's Patti in the middle, looking poised and ready for the seventies—in blue jean *knickers and boots*.

One of the songs presented by Vicki for the new LP nearly caused a knock-down drag-out over its brazen sexual come-on. Patti was not having it; the lyric about preferring, actually *demanding*, sex in the morning was way too audacious. She thought it would alienate the fans who'd come up with the Bluebelles' sound of 1950s-style female primness. Vicki knew Labelle would never reach rock star status without bringing the sexy. Hendrix, Jim Morrison, Jagger, and Sly all knew how to poke the libido, and don't all teens and young adults live vicariously on the edge of rock's provocation to the erotic? In her essay "The Erotic as Power," Audre Lorde examines "the false belief that only by the suppression of the erotic within our lives and consciousness can women be truly strong. But that strength is illusory, for it is fashioned within the context of male models of power."[3] Labelle were on the cusp of presenting a new female model of power—erotic and visionary—through music.

Patti eventually joined Nona and Sarah in unleashing her inner naughty with a song called "Morning Much

Better," a song discovered by Vicki as recorded by Genya Ravan with Ten Wheel Drive. Ravan was formerly the lead singer of Goldie and the Gingerbreads, thought of as the very first women's rock band. Labelle's version opens the LP with an ominous intro indicating "something wicked this way comes." And does it ever. While researching, I asked Vicki for a remembered song from her childhood, and she named "The Teddy Bear's Picnic," the 1932 version by Henry Hall. "If you go down in the woods today, you're sure of a big surprise . . ." The descending notes of that song's intro feature a creeping portent of danger, similar to the theme of *The Alfred Hitchcock Hour*. As all brilliant artists understand, the smaller, seemingly undetectable threads of nuance and color woven into a story make it that much more capable of burrowing into your subconscious.

The opening cut on their debut LP, "Morning Much Better" is straight-up midtempo funk, with the bass, kick drum, and guitar all banging tight together on the foreboding beat. Each bar of the verse ends in a closed hi-hat double spank, and the guitar grabs just enough rockin' *wah-wah* to complement Patti's copperhead-strikes-the-swamp-thing delivery as she sasses her "daddy" about the way he's treating her. And then—BAM—that gospel choir of three ROARS, introducing a new blend; Labelle's sonic rage of love. Nona's and Sarah's voices push Patti toward what she once thought might be a dangerous cliff, now exposed as a fecund garden, theirs to dance, wail, and roll around in. The Muscle Shoals sound of the band is far grittier, more soulful than any music the trio had previously worked with. In Patti's, Nona's, and Sarah's voices, you hear and feel how they've been living for this place, this moment, as we meet the new Labelle in a flagrante delicto of funk. The song keeps building, peaking, with Patti digging into the sexual heat she once felt forbidden to expose. At the song's end, she lets out an a cappella sigh: "Ooooh yeeaah." Time for that cigarette.

The album *Labelle* made me hunger for another platter of the group's sonic goodness. No female vocal group had ever sounded like this, so raw and full of love-sexy fire. And the music: a gumbo infused with gospel and R&B, soul and New Orleans–style blues. It's a good collection of songs, some penned by the greatest songwriters of the day, such as "You've Got a Friend" by Carole King. All three voices sing choruses together and arrange untypical poly-rhythmic parts around the beats and Patti's lead. They rearrange Laura Nyro's "Time and Love" into a rock-gospel opera in miniature. (Nyro was waiting in the wings for her own dance with Labelle.) Other covers include the Rolling Stones' "Wild Horses" and a song once performed by Vicki's pal Long John Baldry called "When the Sun Comes Shining Through." In collaboration with Vicki, Gene Casey, and the musicians, Labelle take the songs apart, rebuilding each with their own unique musical architecture.

Nona and Patti wrote their first song together for this LP; a glimpse of just where this beautiful hot mess was heading. "Shades of Difference" previews future Labellian social commentary with the lines "Hey, we don't care if you fade away, say, we're gonna save the world today," and features the three singers trading leads on the verses and roaring out a three-part on the choruses. "Baby's Out of Sight" is another slowly funked declaration of a missing lover, written by Sarah Dash and Armstead Edwards, Patti's husband. On the Nona Hendryx–penned "Too Many Days," the attempt at funk pales in comparison to the vocal fire. On "Time," cowritten by Patti and Armstead, the band is in rare form on a ballad worthy of a New Orleans night on Rampart Street. You sway in the crowd, feeling it all, letting those notes creep up your spine. Labelle are in their element here to full effect, questioning time as both enemy and friend. Listen for the Hammond B3, humming quietly beneath, and when we hit mid-bridge, the organ rises up in full growl, dancing with the bluesy guitar as the women sing their passion. "Time," "Morning Much Better," and "Shades of Difference" are the standouts on the album *Labelle*. Released in 1971, the LP presented the musical foundation for the group's future. Labelle opened several shows for the Who, expanding their reach to a predominantly white rock audience while supporting their LP. And despite Patti's fears about the new direction, their Black audience thrilled to the changes.

Later in 1971, Vicki, Nona, and Sarah relocated to New York City. Patti remained in Philly with husband Armstead but would travel consistently to record and tour with Nona and Sarah.

One afternoon in New York, Vicki was on her way uptown to interview a singer-songwriter for *Melody Maker*, and Patti asked if she could tag along. The artist was Laura Nyro, and the meeting would launch an extraordinary chapter in the book of Labelle.

– 6 –

CAMPANOLOGY:
J'ENTENDS LES CLOCHES

Labelle and Laura Nyro created the space for
cross-racial feminist thought.

MARK ANTHONY NEAL

As I used to tell Laura all the time, she is a black woman
in a white girl's body.

PATTI LABELLE

To me, singing is the closest thing to flying.

LAURA NYRO

Why are there so few collaborations between Black and
white women musicians? What keeps us on either side of
an imaginary line that only exists because of its projection
on our collective consciousness? Can we think about how
popular musics serve as placeholders for the conquer-and-
divide set, a type of social engineering conducted by those
all too happy to dine out on our separations? I'm not suggesting Black and white collabs by women will rock the

patriarchy off its axis, but a rumble and crack in our musical apartheid sure would be welcome. Mark Anthony Neal posed the what-if of Black and white women musicians working together at the end of his chapter "Bellbottoms, Bluebelles, and the Funky-Ass White Girl."[1] Neal's closing sentence set me to imagining Missy Elliott in the studio with Björk. Or a collaboration between Meshell Ndegeocello and Fiona Apple. Yes to both, and more, please.

A meeting of this kind, one that blew up sonic segregations and elevated girlsong to Olympian heights, took place nearly fifty years ago and, in my opinion, has not happened as magnificently since. Aside from Dusty Springfield's duet with Martha Reeves on *RSG!* in 1965, I could not excavate another instance of Black and white women singing together before Laura Nyro and Labelle came together for *Gonna Take a Miracle*.

When Vicki visited Laura Nyro for that interview, Patti tagged along. According to Patti's account, meeting Nyro was magic, two musical souls joining voices. How did Nyro capture Patti's heart? For one, they knew all the same songs, soul tunes and girl-group tunes. Songs like "Jimmy Mack," "I Met Him on a Sunday," and "You've Really Got a Hold on Me." Patti would never have sung backing vocals for another singer, let alone a white girl. She didn't need to. Labelle were on their way to their own stardom. So what compelled Labelle to join Laura Nyro in the studio for *Gonna Take a Miracle*?

Listen. It's in the grooves. Crank the LP *Gonna Take*

a Miracle and you'll hear one of the greatest musical love affairs on wax. On the back cover of the LP, Laura describes the dance of girlsong in a kind of haiku plus two:

Nights
in New York
        running down steps
                into the echoes of the train station
                                to sing . . .

The daughter of a jazz trumpeter, Bronx girl Laura Nyro developed an extremely idiosyncratic style of playing piano and singing as a child. Her songwriting mixed elements of show tunes, soul, R&B, and rock. Unorthodox progressions, tempos, and movements were created to serve her street-savvy poetry. Patti describes Laura as "a black woman in a white girl's body." I'm half-Sicilian and I take umbrage with the term "blue-eyed soul," a Wonder Bread metaphor often applied to Nyro, who was hardly blue-eyed; her ancestry is Italian and Eastern European Jewish. Hers is the type of voice people either fall in love with or find just too honestly raw, too tonally high; and, truthfully, the same can be said about Patti's voice. The "it" of Nyro's singing that prompts Labelle into the swirl is a certain gravitas, a soulfulness and warmth expressing a deep empathy with the human condition, in joy and in sorrow. It's the sound you hear in a gospel choir, and despite the legacy of suffering that lies at the root of gospel music, and in honor of it, that sound can slip racial boundaries and take root in whatever genetic it chooses to kidnap.

A wildness snakes through the blend of all four women's voices on *Gonna Take a Miracle*, bringing to mind the tradition of Federico García Lorca's *duende*, the mischievous spirit alive in only the bravest of art.[2] You must invite the spirit in (as you would a vampire), opening your deepest wounds so the dance of surrender might commence in the blood and emerge again in your work: much like the animal spirits flowing from the pineal gland, those René Descartes describes as "a very lively and pure flame."[3] Artists like Nyro and Labelle aim for the hurt spot, the wound aching for love with an animal wail we carry and too often bury. A work's greatness is directly tied to our ability to choreograph this dance of pain and pleasure. You are hearing *duende*, pure and raw, on *Gonna Take a Miracle*.

When she met Patti, Nona, and Sarah, Laura was coming off *Christmas and the Beads of Sweat*, the last disc in an amazing trilogy. Along with *New York Tendaberry* and *Eli and the Thirteenth Confession*, the albums form a collection that many view as the peak of Nyro's solo career. But we can't relegate *Gonna Take a Miracle* to less-than-holy status because the songs are covers. The album is a masterpiece, with Labelle having everything to do with its brilliance. It would be the last disc Laura recorded before leaving the music business for a five-year hiatus. She was twenty-four, uncomfortable with the idea of celebrity, and, based on accounts of her life before and post-hiatus, uneasy with her own sexuality.

Gonna Take a Miracle sets up Labelle's future riot of girl-gang glory. In the summer of 1971, Nyro and Labelle entered Sigma Sound Studios in Philadelphia with producers Kenny Gamble and Leon Huff, grand masters of Philly soul. The creators of TSOP—"The Sound of Philadelphia" and the theme song of *Soul Train*—Gamble and Huff also produced dozens of classic hits, such as "Me and Mrs. Jones" by Billy Paul, "Love Train" by the O'Jays, and "When Will I See You Again" by the Three Degrees. (A note about TSOP: Sigma Sound is legendary in the annals of popular music, and the Schubert Building was Philly's equivalent to New York's Brill Building. Leon Huff spent his time between the two songwriting meccas and met his partner, Kenny Gamble, in an elevator at the Schubert. David Bowie recorded his "plastic soul" LP, *Young Americans*, at Sigma Sound. Several of Patti's solo LPs were recorded there, along with LPs by many other musical icons.)

Despite Laura's gorgeous piano playing and the fantastic band, singing is sovereign on this LP. I imagine Gamble and Huff were happy to give the quartet their "echoes of the train station" ambient magic and Philly sound glaze without too much meddling. The vocals for this extraordinary LP of ten songs were recorded in *four and a half hours*. No auto-tuning, no stop-'n'-drop recording on syllables, no digital *Bullenscheiße*. Laura takes the lead here, just as Patti takes the lead on most Labelle tracks, but there is plenty of step-out love going on too with the others. The blend of gorgeous that occurs when those voices come together on *Gonna Take a Miracle* is Labellian, as previewed earlier that same year on their first solo LP. Labelle had an aptitude for creating idiosyncratic vocal arrangements on the fly, and here, in concert with Laura's own musical innovations, I contend it's the first time they have really let loose and gone for it, creating a style we haven't heard from any other female singing group.

The soulfulness of this LP also evolved due to their close friendship. Patti regarded Laura as one of her closest friends, and Nona lived a few blocks away from Laura on New York's Upper West Side. "We would all go over to Laura's, sit around the piano and sing, then eat, then sing some more," Hendryx tells me. "The recording was an extension of what we did at Laura's house." Laura's idiosyncratic style of songwriting helped inspire Nona in learning how to write songs directly tailored to Labelle's strengths. Wikipedia's entry for the LP completely misses the mark with the statement that Laura was "using Labelle as a traditional back-up vocal group." This couldn't be further from the truth. The LP is nothing short of miraculous: about as traditional as a woman winning the presidency.

Every girl and woman should enjoy the camaraderie of a girl gang at least once in their lives. I'm not talking gang in a girl-hoodlum sense, although an art or music girl gang (Guerilla Girls, Pussy Riot) might be considered dangerous, depending. Boy culture begins with boys being taught to play on teams, to have each other's backs. When they compete, it's in the spirit of the team winning. They're never taught to feel there's only room for *one* star player on the basketball court. Women of Labelle's, Vicki's, and Laura's generation were raised to conform to standards of prettiness and propriety: to compete with their girlfriends on looks and on landing Mr. Right. For *Gonna Take a Miracle*, Labelle and Nyro left female competition outside the studio door. You will not find a moment on this LP of one singer attempting to outshine the others.

I had fallen in love with Nyro and Labelle when I first entered the gay underground of Cleveland at seventeen, in 1972. Finally able to work (in order to buy records!), I purchased a copy of *Gonna Take a Miracle* and was astonished: a white girl singing with three Black girls central enough to the songs that the artist states right up front on the album sleeve, Laura Nyro *with* Labelle. Turn the album cover over: on the back, three women gaze out from the gloss. Their hair is natural. They wear black turtlenecks and expressions of confidence and authority, smiles unnecessary while reflecting their own *Meet the Beatles!* moment. A force to be reckoned with. Hardly your ordinary backing singers, their eyes speak: *We are not here pandering to anyone's vision of how we should sound. Or look. Or live. Listen. Throw open your windows, girl, and listen.*

I've never stopped listening. The voices shot off sparks

of hope through the darkness of my singularity. After leaving Blossom Hill, I felt utterly out of place in most social groups. At parties or gatherings in gay segregated Cleveland, Black folks' initial reaction of *What the hell is this little white girl doing here?* usually about-faced into *What? She can sing!* That the Black cooks and cottage guards at Blossom Hill were being paid to look after me might have mattered to them, but I never felt ignored or ostracized. There was kindness and big belly laughs. Comfort food and music. Aside from my grandmother (whose racial mix was always cryptic), Black women and girls nurtured me more than any white person or family member ever had, and music was the source of that nourishment. Music, ever and always. Here's where my lifelong fascination with alchemy returns; cook the experiences of life down into a reduction, add more music, stir, and your roux becomes the sweet essence of kindred.

Gonna Take a Miracle was the first time I'd hear white and Black women singing together outside of Blossom Hill. Years after Laura and Labelle threw down in the studio, Donna Summer teamed up with Barbra Streisand for "No More Tears (Enough Is Enough)," Annie Lennox joined Aretha for "Sisters Are Doin' It for Themselves," and Gwen Stefani partnered with Eve on "Rich Girl," and that's about it to date, as far as I can tell.

The record is much more than a tribute to the golden era of the girl group. If Laura and Labelle intended to weave a spell of musical witchcraft, they succeeded. The

LP begins with the rubric of girlsong; the a cappella voices of Laura, Patti, Nona, and Sarah singing "I Met Him on a Sunday (Ronde-Ronde)." Written and originally sung by the Shirelles, it's a key song of the girl-group genre and the first release to defy the passive paradigm of female desperation by fronting on a guy for being late to a date. When the Bluebelles auditioned for their first record deal, Patti recalls singing "I Met Him on a Sunday." The song cradles the essence of the girl-group sound. You hear the rocking of handclap games, finger-snapping, harmonies, and double Dutch roundelay rhymes: a fitting intro to an LP that magnifies the beauty of the girl-gang route from playground to microphone. It also dignifies girl-group singers, the ones who've slipped through history without acknowledgment of their value to our musical culture.

I remember the good chill I felt when I first heard those a cappella voices switching lines on "I Met Him on a Sunday." Midsong, Laura sings "Bye-bye baby," her jubilant piano kicking in with cowbell and bass and Labelle's harmonics on the "doo ron de ronde ronde." *Yep, bye-bye baby, it's all about the girls now.* After this foreplay, I was primed for the best musical lay of my life (I admit: I'm a melolagniac). It happened on the next track, "The Bells."

The last *ooohs* of "I Met Him on a Sunday" slip into Laura's solo intro to "The Bells," a Marvin Gaye song cowritten with his wife, Anna Gordy. As the song builds toward the bridge and Laura asks, "Can you hear the bells ringing when I'm kissing you?" is she serenading her "Désiree," from track five of the LP? Is Désiree answering through Patti, affirming, "I hear the bells"? If it doesn't sound like two women singing their passion to one another warmed by the fire of Nona's and Sarah's voices, stick a fork in me, for I am crackle. Young queers coming of age in the early 1970s were desperate for the tiniest sliver of love and validation. We'd take a fine-tooth comb to a haystack searching for a strand of queer. The woman-love of 1971's *Gonna Take a Miracle* wasn't just critically downplayed, it was profoundly unacknowledged. But we queer girls were listening.

Martha Reeves and the Vandellas' music has an earthy, gritty vitality and would be Nyro's choice for the songs on this record. (The pop prissiness of the Supremes couldn't hang with this suite.) Labelle's vocals contain a spin of the unexpected holler better suited to songs like "Dancing in the Street" and "Nowhere to Run." It's on the two Vandella songs where the jams turn political. (Mark Anthony Neal speaks eloquently to how these two tracks have been lengthened and reshaped toward a new perception.) "Dancing in the Street" is a mash-up that starts with the Curtis Mayfield–penned "Monkey Time." Shifting gears into "Dancing . . . ," things really start to cook, the loose pocket groove of the arrangement and the voices creating a total celebration, paying homage to the spirit of Motown and the Detroit riots—in fact, to all the riots of the late 1960s and the thrill of rebellion unleashed. In the voices of Laura and Labelle, the song becomes a paean to music and dance as expressions of pride and resistance and, through collaboration, a musical symbol of Black and white unity. *Amandla!* "This is an invitation across the nation, a chance for folks to meet . . ."

The song cracks into a breakdown of drums and bass, the voices all demanding we "don't forget the Motor City," united in harmony, singing a strident unison ad-lib on "I said it looks to me like this could be . . ." and Laura punches in with "Motor City!" The track is a masterpiece.

Laura follows with the ethereal "Désiree," the first time I'd hear a woman singing a love song to another woman. Unlike "The Bells," also easily imagined as a song of love between women, "Désiree" sweeps in softly like an erotic prayer. Laura Nyro met young Maria Desiderio in 1967, allegedly through Alice Coltrane (Nyro's friend and neighbor, Coltrane was teaching piano lessons at the time) when Maria was a mere thirteen years old. On the back cover of *Eli and the Thirteenth Confession*, released in 1968, we see Laura in silhouette kissing the forehead of a younger woman, making it hardly a stretch to read "Désiree" as Laura's serenade and promise to her future partner. "You've Really Got a Hold on Me" follows, another song about the kind of love you want to run away from but can't. Labelle echoes back every nuance of emotion in Nyro's voice, especially in the erotic love gasps after the chorus lines of "All I want you to do . . . ," Labelle drawing out the notes on "hold" and Laura answering "tighter." And on goes the love play. Sexy stuff. Patti mirrors Laura's ache when she wails over four bars into the last verse, and Laura shifts into an up-tempo roll on the vamp out, each voice expressing longing, coming together at the end in harmony.

There are other sweet, soulful renditions here, of "Spanish Harlem" and "Jimmy Mack." It's a polyamorous love-fest between Laura and Labelle all the way through. "The Wind," an ethereal tune about a missing lover, precedes the phenomenal "Nowhere to Run," which starts with Labelle singing the signature line and Laura joining as lead, with Patti, Nona, and Sarah breaking into three-part harmony. Just another song in the vein of captivity to a forbidden love? But as the song unfolds and shifts into the drive section of a gospel improv, there's something else going on here, several themes that Nyro and Labelle's pentimento wash of sound can't disguise. The music shifts, then drops out, and the song goes full-on gospel a cappella, with fired-up handclaps and tambourines as all four women chant-sing, "No no, ain't got nowhere to run to!" Labelle sound utterly defiant. Nyro dances in and out of their chant, alternating notes of melancholy, resignation, and anger. Lying beneath this dance of female voices, the skin Labelle can't run from, nor should they wish to. Nyro might be able to "hide" her true love inside a white hetero mask, but for how long? And at what cost? Her passion for another woman in a homophobic society (let alone a homo-hating music business that nearly drove so many artists to suicide) and the rage of love that is Labelle dance free in this song. A conversation between the forbidden and the defiant, both longing for release, calls to us from the grooves.

The LP closes with the title track, "Gonna Take a Miracle," a fairly straightforward rendering of the song elevated by the beautiful vocal blend and the song's sentiment of being forever transformed by an encounter with love. No singer would walk away from this project unaltered.

When Patti struggled with postpartum depression after the birth of her son, it was Laura who rushed to her side. Nona says Laura Nyro was "almost like another member of Labelle, like family." Labelle would begin recording *Moon Shadow* after working with Nyro, carrying the spirit of *Gonna Take a Miracle*'s accomplishment and its message into Nona's writing and the LP's recording sessions.

After recording with Labelle, Laura ran. Left the music business to hide out with her new husband, Gil Bianchi, in what she hoped would be the same type of warmth she discovered in the women-centered friendships and relationships inside and around Labelle. But Nyro's marriage was short-lived. She would give birth to a son by another man before reconnecting with her soul mate, Maria Desiderio. The two women spent the last seventeen years of Nyro's life together until her untimely death of ovarian cancer in 1997.

Laura Nyro passed away on my birthday, April 8, and every year on that day I play "The Bells," imagining the four women singing and laughing together, the excitement of their joined voices bringing shivers.

Laura Nyro performed at Carnegie Hall in late 1971. She brought Labelle out for an encore, and they sang "The Wind," "Dancing in the Street," and "The Bells" together, accompanied only by Laura's piano, and the audience lost their minds.[4] To have heard these women's voices together filling that hall live, to even imagine it, takes my breath away. The show's audio was crudely recorded, yet despite the lousy tech, you can feel the thrill of the moment. Finding themselves onstage at Carnegie Hall was a big deal for Labelle at the time, but they'd grace the same boards soon as headliners in 1973. And in '74, they would become the first contemporary vocal act to play New York's Metropolitan Opera House.

Gonna Take a Miracle knocked a hole in the wall of musical apartheid. Together, Laura and Labelle stepped through to bring us an LP of astonishing beauty and love, songs that serenade us with a promise of new understandings . . . shimmering right there at the edge of song. One of music's holiest gifts? Its immortality. Listen. You can still hear them in that Philly studio, singing to each other and to us across the misconceived divide.

– 7 –

REVOLUTION, TELEVISED

Labelle recorded their sophomore LP, *Moon Shadow*, produced by Vicki Wickham and Jack Adams, at New York's Record Plant in 1972. The LP's story begins with the cover. Labelle hang out on a boardwalk bench, claiming their public space betwixt a gaggle of old white guys. With their attitudes, fedoras, and overcoats, the men could be Italian Americans, suggesting the album cover is a reference to long-standing racial tensions between Italian Americans and African Americans. Patti's hands are crossed over her purse and lap, and it appears less about protecting her goods than it is about mimicking the same pose as her benchmates. The men at the far right engage in whispers while Nona and Sarah look on, smiles signaling, *This is our space too, and we're claiming it*. Sarah shows thigh-high leg in a foreshadowing of the sexual brazenness soon to turn Labelle into a household name.

Labelle play around on *Moon Shadow*, stretching out, taking new risks. The title song written by Cat Stevens is given a funkified revamp, with solo step-outs from all three singers and the musicians on an extended ride of nine minutes plus. I'm partial to Hammond B3s and Wurlitzers, and the organ work from Andre "Mandré" Lewis shines all over this LP. He really goes off on "Moonshadow." The song turns cornball though, singing us through the loss of each body part. A song they would premiere on the public television show *Soul!*, "I Believe That I've Finally Made It Home" is a Nona composition, a strong indication of the "personal is political" songs she'd write for Labelle going forward. Sarah makes a written contribution too—"Peace with Yourself," a solid gospel rocker—but aside from "Moonshadow" and "Won't Get Fooled Again," Nona is credited with the remaining songs here. "Touch Me All Over" is a beautifully arranged ballad, and the whispering harmony of voices singing the intro together slays. Nona's songs on *Moon Shadow* show how musically astute she can be when writing for Patti's voice, and for their three voices together. Nona was building an inimitable songwriting style in the tradition of writers like Curtis Mayfield and Laura Nyro.

That Labelle is ripping away the mask of propriety while taking on hypocrisy is most evident on "People Say They're Changing." The song starts with some dirty clav(inet) courtesy of Mandré, and Patti steps in to the music with a wail. Hendryx writes,

> Uncle Tom, they tell me he passed away
> Overheard, he's resting for another day

Friends will come and pull him from his grave
Because deep down in every heart, there's a master and
    a slave.

The trio's intentions for truth telling shine on *Moon Shadow*. Not that Labelle didn't feel the love songs of their earlier incarnation; they could never have delivered such stellar vocal performances had they not. But truth would be essential from here on out, with love underscoring all.

In Harlem, epicenter of the Black Arts Movement, which writer Larry Neal describes as the "aesthetic and spiritual sister of the Black Power concept," poet Nikki Giovanni became a leading voice among many influential women all writing to power; among them, Audre Lorde, Maya Angelou, Gwendolyn Brooks, and Sonia Sanchez. Giovanni herself was a Labelle fan, and Nona began writing to the theorem of the Black Arts Movement. Her confidence as a writer flourished in this environment. With Vicki and their new label as support, Labelle finally felt free to shake off the "little white man that sits on your shoulder"—the one James Baldwin discussed with Toni Morrison. About this censorious critic, Morrison says, "So, I wanted to knock him off, and you're free. Now I own the world. I mean, I can write about anything, to anyone, for anyone."[1] The Black Arts Movement helped Labelle realize they could give up the struggle for inclusion in pop music and choose to tell the truth, no matter the consequence. It was time.

Patti, Nona, and Sarah were in attendance (right beside

Nina Simone) at the Canaan Baptist Church where Nikki Giovanni broke new ground, performing her word magic backed by the gospel glory of Benny Diggs's New York Community Choir. Shortly after, Labelle joined Nikki onstage for a Father's Day concert at Canaan on June 18, 1972. They joined her again a month later at Alice Tully Hall, Lincoln Center, for the Ellis Haizlip–produced sixteen-part series *Soul at the Center.* When I spoke with Nikki Giovanni about Labelle as players in the Black Arts Movement, she recounted how everyone in the Harlem scene had been listening to Patti LaBelle and the Blue-belles from day one, attending their shows at the Apollo. Giovanni told me, "Labelle brought the love, the joy. They brought the people to the dance floor."

Giovanni's spoken-word poetry backed by a gospel choir was an inspiration to the singers, helping to inform Labelle's sound, individuating through Nona's lyrical melding of politics set to a wild gospel blend. When Giovanni recorded the brilliant LP *Truth Is on Its Way*, Labelle was in the house: hear them singing on the track "Alabama Poem."

I recently heard musician Brian Eno speaking about the waste we make of cooperative intelligence. He spoke of how we single out individual artists as geniuses, the important ones, without much acknowledgment of the scenes they were immersed in and inspired by. Most people we raise up as geniuses thrived within flourishing cultural scenes, be it 1920s Paris, the Beat Generation, Weimar, the Harlem

Renaissance, and so forth. Eno calls this "scenius": "Just as genius is the creative intelligence of an individual, scenius is the creative intelligence of a community."[2] The Black Arts Movement was such a community. In 1977 after Labelle broke up, Nona became a fixture in another scenius: downtown New York's new wave, no wave, punk-funky dance explosion.

A televised reflection of the Black Arts Movement, *Soul!* was an hour-long variety show broadcast on NYC's PBS station, WNET. It debuted in 1968, with Patti LaBelle and the Bluebelles performing for its inaugural episode. *Soul!* was the first TV show to present Black cultural pride and power across a spectrum of entertainment and politics. A hit in New York and picked up for syndication across seventy-two cities, *Soul!*'s Black audience finally felt represented in truth and power, on television. The show and its guests provoked an in-depth consideration of Black culture and its social impact at a convulsive time in America's conversation about race. *Soul!* was as much a fulcrum to the movement as Harlem was its epicenter.

Soul!'s visionary producer and presenter Ellis Haizlip dismissed the concept of "high and low" culture, presenting an inclusive place where the opera singer Marian Anderson shared space with Stokely Carmichael and Redd Foxx. Musicians and singers had to play live, no singing to backing tracks like on *American Bandstand*. Various guests included Betty Shabazz, Pharoah Sanders, Sidney Poitier, Esther Phillips, Muhammad Ali, and the Last Poets. Nikki

Giovanni and Jerry Butler hosted several shows featuring music performances and unexpected conversations: Toni Morrison with Jr. Walker and the All Stars (Morrison read from her debut novel, *The Bluest Eye*), Jesse Jackson in conversation with singer Merry Clayton. Among the most riveting are two hour-length shows featuring a discussion between Giovanni and James Baldwin, who said, "What the world does to you, if the world does it to you long enough and effectively enough, you begin to do to yourself."[3] Producer Haizlip's guests often spoke to this need to escape from the colonizer and the self-colonized mind through art and activism. It's a message we'll hear resonating in Labelle's future work.

Sarah tells me Labelle performed on *Soul!* so many times that people started referring to it as the "Labelle and Ellis Haizlip Show," and Nona speaks of Ellis in near worshipful tones today.

A Labelle performance stands out from November of 1972, when they debuted songs from *Moon Shadow* on the special "Shades of Soul Part II." Unfortunately, host Jerry B. screws up and misnames Patti as Trisha Edwards(?) during the intro, but that sure didn't deter Patti. Warning: this performance is flammable, so hydrate well before watching.[4]

They begin the set with Nona's "I Believe That I've Finally Made It Home." The lyric announces their final liberation from handcuffed passivity: they greet a space where groupthink is kicked to the curb as the whole "political world has gone insane." Where truth and new conceptions of a way to be in the world sing from "home," as in home is where the heart *and* the pride is. When Nona sings, "Good morning, friends and relations, I know you thought you were being kind when you locked up my mind," she could be singing about the radical creative changes the women were going through and the possible effect they had on family and friends. Patti's vocal confidence on this song belies her earlier protestations about taking risks. Singing this new material is liberating in and of itself. What made it feel even better? They were finally seeing advance payments from their record company and better pay for their live dates. Instead of Patti fitting in, we sense her willingness to stand out, to follow her own advice as stated in one of her books decades later: "Women who want to lead the orchestra have to turn their back on the crowd."[5]

Soul!'s studio audience shows big love at the end of Labelle's first song. All three singers have broken a sweat, and here's where things go erotically funky. A seductive love song of Nona's, "Touch Me All Over," starts off slow and sexy, the organ creeping in around Patti's first notes. She's moan-wailing the need embedded in the song's lyric, and she's nowhere near the microphone, yet diva is loud enough to be heard over bombs. Bending at the waist, feeling it, lips open in a silent scream, she makes the studio audience erupt without a single vowel leaving her lips. She does a few gospel hops and wing flaps, moves she'll become famous for later and what some fans call her "chicken dance." (Patti's moves become wilder with the years . . . when a song jumps the track from throat into assorted muscles, she'll kick off her heels toward Mars, thrashing into a drop 'n' roll on the stage floor . . . she *goes there*, unafraid to set her inner bad girl free. Pure *duende*.)

The singers follow with Nina Simone's "Four Women." All three get into it, acting out the nuances of Simone's characters, and this is a performance where Sarah Dash shines, embodying the Aunt Sarah of Simone's story. Nona portrays Saffronia, the sophisticated high-yellow girl, representing the character to a T, and Patti is Sweet Thing, giving hip shakes and sass. The three come together as one in character number four, singing in unity, and when they stop the band at the end to sing a cappella and you hear the harmonic pain of that last line, Labelle is Peaches; is a woman you do not want to mess with. They close the set with a deeply funky version of the Who's "Won't Get Fooled Again," a message not lost on an audience now out of their seats, dancing, applauding, and singing along.

Ellis Haizlip's *Soul!* continued to air until the spring of 1973, thanks to a grant from the Ford Foundation. Still, the show would eventually prove too much for those gatekeepers concerned with the social engineering of American culture. In her book *It's Been Beautiful: "Soul!" and Black Power Television*, Gayle Wald describes how the Corporation for Public Broadcasting changed its policies when Nixon took over the reins from President Johnson, the latter having created PBS when he was in office. It seems *Soul!* was transmitting a little too much Black pride and power, causing the top execs at the Corporation for Public Broadcasting to decide that shows of its kind were "hindrances to racial progress." FBI boss J. Edgar Hoover directed his COINTELPRO division to covertly neutralize the Black power movement. Under his and Nixon's paranoid eyes, it's surprising that *Soul!* continued to air as long as it did.

If Hoover thought the Black Panther Party and their free-breakfast program was the USA's most dangerous internal threat, what must he have thought of Ellis Haizlip's show? *Soul!* was danger quadrupled. Haizlip might not have come out on national television, but he didn't exactly hide his sexuality. Imagine: Black, proud, gay, on TV with a syndicated show presenting Black music, art, and political and intellectual discourse airing in seventy-two cities across the country in the early 1970s. White politicians and entertainment executives must have messed their power panties. The Corporation for Public Broadcasting threw down the gauntlet: Haizlip would integrate the show or face cancellation. Haizlip wouldn't compromise. The last show aired in the spring of 1973. *Soul!* might have ended, but its guests continued to grow a movement in activism, music, literature, and the arts. Labelle got busy cooking up their own revolution with their next (and only) LP for RCA Records, *Pressure Cookin'*.

Patti gave birth to her son, Zuri, in July of 1973. She performed throughout her pregnancy but always chose to spend as much time as possible in Philly, while Nona and Sarah were investigating other interests in NYC. Nona was discovering French new wave and Italian film (she's a Fellini fan) while checking out writers Henry Miller, Ram Dass, T. S. Eliot, Nina Simone, and Gil Scott-Heron. Sarah was reading about dreams and altered consciousness, themes we'll encounter in future Labelle songs. Both she and Nona were intrigued by cybernetics, the functions and processes of goal-oriented systems that we now associate with the transhumanism of cyborgs, robotics, and AI. All of these influences, including Patti's new motherhood, informed the visions for future sonic journeys.

Before the internet, before television, radio, newspapers, before can-and-string, poets traveled from village to village bringing the news in song. The tradition of the griot— troubadour and storyteller—came to the Caribbean by way of West Africans kidnapped and brought to work on the sugar plantations of Trinidad. By the mid-nineteenth century, Trinidadian calypso blended African semaphoric rhythms and harmonics with storytelling, and griots beget *chantuelles* beget calypsonians: the poets and singers of news. Islanders relied on calypsonians to provide political satire and an entertaining respite from the colonizers. Like the protest songs of the 1960s in the United States, calypso was of and for the people, a more honest and humorous reportage than the dry and suspect "news" delivered via journalists and politicians. Nona channeled *griotte* energy in the songs she wrote for *Pressure Cookin'*, a tradition she'd continue throughout her career with Labelle and as a solo artist. Old-school pressure cookers have a "jiggle top," a weighted pressure regulator that sits on top of the lid's vent pipe. There's a release button on the cover, and when that jiggle top starts dancing, you'd better release the steam slowly. Neglect the pot, and the pressure builds up, causing the seal to fail . . . and the pot explodes.

Political assassinations, racism, Vietnam, and Watergate stoked the maelstrom of American crazy in the late 1960s and early '70s. We turned to our musical poets for solace, to help us sort out the tangle of collective heartbreak. And did they deliver! The griot(te) called to us through the voices of Marvin Gaye, Bob Dylan, Curtis Mayfield, Joan Baez, Gil Scott-Heron, Nina Simone, Stevie Wonder, Sly and the Family Stone, Laura Nyro, and Crosby, Stills, Nash, and Young. Protest in song influenced Nona's songwriting and Labelle's presentation. Marvin Gaye's *What's Going On* and *Trouble Man*, Mayfield's *Superfly*, Stevie's *Innervisions*, George Clinton and Funkadelic's *Maggot Brain* and "You and Your Folks": these LPs and songs were the inner-city soundtracks of 1973. (Coincidentally, Clinton was a barber in Plainfield, New Jersey, and used to cut Nona's hair at the Silk Palace barbershop years before either of them ascended into space-time.)

With *Pressure Cookin'*, Labelle established their place among the firmament of America's most significant radical music groups. It is the only LP released in 1973 to hold equal weight with the fellas, female-band style, in terms of righteous message and musical innovation. And like the boy bands of the British Invasion, most of whom wrote their own songs and didn't need to depend on outside writers, Labelle was becoming self-contained via Nona's songwriting and Vicki's management.

Nona's songs were not just socially conscious; the lyrics expressed love alongside rage—an emotion women have been forbidden to reveal or express, and when we do, we're bitches, punished and shamed for speaking out against BS and injustice. *Shame* is a word you won't find in the Labellian lexicon. And when it comes to relationships, Nona does not play with the tired romantic tropes of the 1960s Bluebelles. The new love songs offer the point of view of strong, full-blooded women who can be vulnerable while knowing what they want and need, and exactly how to get it.

The LP kicks in with a warning: "Pressure cookin' . . ." and the groove suddenly stops. Patti wails, "Keep the lid oonnn! Keep it on!" inside the pause. That wail is what Wesley Morris calls Patti's "emotional police siren,"[6] reflecting the racial tensions of the day.

The musicianship is stellar on *Pressure Cookin'*. Playing with tensions, playing to story, all musicians perform in full support of the vocal dazzle. Too many stars to name, but a few stand out as returning players, tossing their skills into a hybridiculous gumbo of soul, rock, funk, and Latin magic. Helping to make this LP a cult classic is returning keyboard player and multi-instrumentalist Andre Lewis a.k.a. Mandré, cocredited with Labelle as having arranged all but two songs (the latter arranged by "a friend"). I think Ben Zebulon plays congas on the first two tracks, supplying the rhythmic torque burned into those grooves, the congas pushing the songs into new registers of Afro-Latin heat.

This time around, Mandré brings along Maxayn, the seriously underrated rock-funk band he shared with singer Maxayn Lewis. Mandré and company give *Pressure Cookin'* a raw street sound missing from Labelle's previous discs.

Vicki Wickham is as comfortable behind a mixing desk as she is negotiating tricky record deals. How many women music producers can you name today? The credits here state, "Produced by Vicki Wickham (*and friend)" (that friend being Stevie Wonder, whose contract with Tamla Motown prevented him from being credited as producer at the time). On the cover, the group's name appears in ornate art deco lettering, with Nona, Sarah, and Patti performing against a black background, all wearing what looks like Norma Kamali: cowl, feathers, winged sleeves. Indications of sartorial mytho-feminism to come. Flip to the back cover: dramatic photos of each woman singing appear with liner notes, a poetic riff on bells written by Nikki Giovanni. In many ways, *Pressure Cookin'* encapsulates the sound of the Black Arts Movement. Labelle's courage is on display and gaining steam.

I'd like to point out that Labelle and Wickham have always honored the guys who've supported their musical journey. Track two brings us back to fairy godfather Kit Lambert and the Who's Pete Townshend. The two are responsible for creating the group Thunderclap Newman and the 1969 post-flower-child anthem "Something in the Air," a song the Labelle team were inspired to mash up with Gil Scott-Heron's "The Revolution Will Not Be Televised." The result is an intersectional sonic boom, blowing up the impossibilities of Black meeting white in a radical remix . . . although we never heard it on the radio. Ever. It's a track that broke my eighteen-year-old mind back then (women can sound like *this*?) and feels as relevant today as it did in 1973. All three singers throw down righteous sass as they take turns with Scott-Heron's poetic scald. My favorite Scott-Heron lyrical moment here arrives courtesy Sarah Dash and two popular hillbilly TV shows: "Hooterville and Petticoat Junction will not be so goddamned relevant!" Gets me every time.

The super-tight funk groove of "Sunshine" begins with some sexy *wah-wah* guitar licks courtesy of Mandré. Nona and Sarah both hold back here in support of Patti, but they'll come together on the choruses. Labelle is learning how to work with pauses in the music, to great effect. Ironically, "Sunshine" is the perfect feel-good song to blast from your car on a warm summer night. The horn arrangements know just where to punch, with a foreshadowing of the Big Easy atmosphere soon to come.

The next track beckons us in like a fairy tale. After the intro of Mandré's vibes brushed with reverb-soaked delay, Nona sings to a missing Bluebelle on "Can I Speak to You Before You Go to Hollywood?," a warning of fame's capricious nature and, inside the caution, a love abiding. Labelle serenade themselves into closure over the loss of Cindy Birdsong in this one; her abrupt departure with no word of goodbye had left the band gutted, and the song warns of the fickle nature of Hollywood's star-making machinery. Sarah holds the spotlight here, and it's well deserved. A warning, a gentle scold, and then Patti comes full-on into the chorus: "Because I believe in you . . . hope all your dreams come true." "Can I Speak to You Before You Go to Hollywood?" is one of few songs written about the love contained in female friendships: love employed as action to break up the aloneness that accompanies female competition.

Stevie Wonder (the credited "friend") contributed a song here too, the swampy strut of "Open Up Your Heart," and he coproduced what should have been a hit single for Labelle, a funk song Nona wrote called "Goin' on a Holiday." David Mancuso gave this dance-worthy funk a good spin at his (and New York City's) beloved Loft, thought of as the birthplace of disco. RCA released "Open Up Your Heart" as the single, because hey, it's Stevie, and the song was a perfect vehicle for Labelle's blend. The Nona original "Goin' on a Holiday" was demoted as the B side, but it should have been the single. Its classic funk groove and lyric moved the behind and the mind, as resonant now as it was in '73. I imagine the white execs at RCA balking at what to do with these *griotte* queens and the politically charged jazz-funky fusion that is *Pressure Cookin'*.

The record business was notoriously sexist in the 1970s. Nearly fifty years later, the same old beauty-bias model remains intact. The majority of execs at the major labels were the gangster-gatekeepers of culture, choosing the music we listened to, knowing full well how music shapes and affects how a society views itself and each other. RCA was the house that Elvis built: Elvis, whose first major hit was an appropriation of a song first snarled and whipped onto wax by a queer Black woman (Big Mama Thornton). RCA signed David Bowie and helped break his career with *The Rise and Fall of Ziggy Stardust and the Spiders from Mars*, and Nina Simone released the brilliant live LP *Emergency Ward!* on RCA in 1972. Maybe this accounts for Wickham thinking RCA might be the perfect match for a force like Labelle.

But all that Black female voltage made this particular ball of wax too hot to handle for RCA. They dropped Labelle and all promo for the LP, but the LP took on its own critical steam. *Pressure Cookin'* would be one among too many criminal oversights on the part of a music industry afraid to support the music of outspoken women.

— 8 —

AFRONAUTICFUTURISTIC-
FUNKADIVALICIOUS

A quick glance at the pop charts of 1974 reveals a penchant for love songs; political songs had lost favor in boardrooms and on radio playlists after 1970, when we heard Edwin Starr's "War" followed by Joni Mitchell's "Big Yellow Taxi" (the latter a scalding diss on environmental destruction cloaked in a sunny, upbeat earworm). Roberta Flack's sublime duets with Donny Hathaway replaced the Roberta of "Compared to What," and Nina Simone stood alone in that Black power space for a moment, addressing the people with her stunning live LP *Black Gold*.

White women I knew were listening to lesbionic "wimmin's" music: Holly Near, Meg Christian, and Alix Dobkin. The peace movement and the women's movement intertwined in these songs, with acoustic guitars strumming smooth progressions for a tame, nonthreatening sameness; a music that felt warm and kind, intending to comfort. Women certainly did need comforting, but this music did not appeal to Black women. Or to me, no disrespect intended. Where was the fire? The anger that both Black and white working-class women forced down in order to survive in an unjust world? In rock and roll, June Millington had guitar skills, but the all-girl band Fanny did not take rebellious risks like Bowie's "Lady Stardust," Marvin Gaye's *What's Going On*, or what I imagined as Sly and the Family Stone's response to Gaye, *There's a Riot Goin' On*. Personally, in the early 1970s I craved a rock and soul rebellion, girl-style. The crunchy guitars and lyrical inanity of "48 Crash" and "Can the Can" didn't change my opinion that listening to Suzi Quatro was akin to grubbing for slugs. The white girls I knew liked her merely because she looked hot in black leather and played a strap-on. (Bass, that is.) We needed a substantial meal to fill up all our empty. Where were the rule breakers, the wailers of convictions? To my ears, the artists igniting feminist musical fires in the 1970s were Black: Aretha, Tina Turner, Betty Davis, Betty Wright, and Joyce "Baby Jean" Kennedy, lead singer of the mixed-race, mixed-genre band Mother's Finest. Without hits, Davis and Kennedy didn't ascend to pop music's firmament, but Labelle must have been aware of and inspired by the bold statements and sexuality of these divas.

In 1974, Labelle were about to top the charts with an Afronautic rage of love. While critics had raved about *Pressure Cookin'* and its genre-blasting funk, Latin, rock, R&B, and soul, RCA had failed miserably with promotion. Not to be deterred, Labelle refurbished their arsenal with provocative songs and performance ideas, while Vicki negotiated a new record deal with execs Gregg Geller and Don Ellis at Epic Records. The Pointer Sisters had hit in 1973 with "Yes We Can Can," no doubt easing the way for another less traditional girl group. Geller suggested that Allen Toussaint (who wrote "Yes We Can Can") produce Labelle's next LP. He hardly had to convince. Toussaint was the Paul Prudhomme of the musical soul banquet that is New Orleans —a perfect match for Labelle's vocal prowess and their new direction.

Before their date with destiny à la Maestro Toussaint, Labelle flew to LA to do a quick show. They were staying at the Sunset Marquis, a rock hedonist heaven in the 1970s. On any given day (or wee hour of the morning) you might see Keith Richards or Bob Marley hanging around the pool, or Keith Moon driving a motorcycle through the lobby where Labelle and Vicki ran into their acquaintance Bob Crewe, who happened to live next door. He invited them over. Another gay contributor to Labelle's success story, Crewe was a songwriter with the pop-magic touch. He'd written a string of hits for Frankie Valli and the Four Seasons ("Walk Like a Man" and "Can't Take My Eyes Off You" among them) and for many other top acts of the 1960s and '70s. With the drink flowing and Labelle gathered around his piano, Crewe played a song he'd written in New Orleans. He'd recorded the song with a disco group called the Eleventh Hour, but the track fell flat. Crewe lacked the lead vocal sass to make the queen of his story come alive, and his instincts about Labelle were on target. It's impossible to imagine any group better suited for Crewe's song. With all its fabulosity and Baz Luhrmann glitz, the *Moulin Rouge!* remake doesn't come close.

"Lady Marmalade" is the story of a Creole hooker strutting a solicitation: "Voulez-vous coucher avec moi, ce soir?" The phrase became a French-language primer for every American in love with pop music. Patti swears she was never told the translation and had no idea what the song was about until after it became a hit. Not to question Patti's honesty, but let's face it, the remaining English lyrics literally scream the tale. And who is Lady Marmalade, really? Crewe suggests a queer spin on Lady M., and ambiguity sits within these grooves: a hooker isn't usually referred to as "Lady."

Was there a conspiracy among Nona, Sarah, and the songwriting team of Crewe and Kenny Nolan to keep Patti in the dark? If Patti was nervous about Labelle losing their Black audience before this, how would they react to hearing Patti in character as a New Orleans street ho? I bet Patti knew. And after her initial shock, the piano ringing out the chords beneath Nona and Sarah's "Gitchee gitchee, ya ya, da da" (Get ya sex here, Daddy!), she couldn't contain herself and just had to ultra-funk a hooker strut to perfection. The *gitchee*s and *mocha-choca-lata*s are street-slang come-ons from the hue of the woman offering her wares. And the *ya-ya*s? Sex. Or ta-tas. Could be either, as in the Rolling Stones' *Get Yer Ya-Ya's Out!* In the time slot between the rebirth of the Bluebelles and Lady Marmalade's appearance,

Patti had learned a valuable lesson: sometimes the craziest ideas are the ones most likely to succeed.

If there was record company trepidation around releasing this brazen shout-out for women's sexual agency to the listening world, any fears must have been extinguished by the undeniable brilliance of the recording. The era of sexy blues sirens like Ma Rainey, Bessie Smith, Billie Holiday, and others was followed by the erotic sass of Eartha Kitt, the deep sensuality of Nina Simone, and the wildness of Tina Turner and Betty Davis née Mabry. The time was ripe for Black women to assert their sexual agency in a new presentation of rock star ferocity.

Prostitution has been around since the matriarchies of 10,000 BCE, with prostitute-priestesses holding court in the temples of Mesopotamia. Eventually the Old Testament dons succeeded in demonizing any woman whose sexuality would not be controlled by men. Nickie Roberts's fascinating book *Whores in History: Prostitution in Western Society* tells of the medieval Catholic Church in Europe actually pimping the prostitutes, demanding that a tax on each horizontal transaction be deposited into the church's coffers. Having unsuccessfully attempted to control their numbers, the Vatican realized it was better to take a percentage from the business of sex work, also inflating the rents on the brothels in "the system of licensing and direct taxation of whores introduced by the syphilitic Pope Sixtus IV in 1471."[1] Prostitutes in many ancient societies were the most learned women of their time. Wives and daughters were not allowed to read or engage in discourse aside from that related to domestic duties, but the higher class of prostitute didn't merely sex her clients: she engaged in conversation and dialogue about world affairs and, possibly, read books for a view outside the brothel, through a locked window that could only be shattered by the seizing of sexual agency.

There are so many layers to "Lady Marmalade." The song might not have been written by Labelle, but their delivery laid a 100 percent claim to making it a worldwide sensation. Both Sarah and Nona say they knew the song was a hit at first listen. Slower than the usual 120–135 bpm of disco, it's a gut-bucket New Orleans strut decorated in the glamour of Toussaint's arrangements, the hermetic musical language of New Orleans. Bayou disco-funk played with a musical sophistication that makes you feel the humidity in the room where Labelle and the players threw down. Funk before this had never been topped by a triadic gospel wail.

Another musical signature identifying these singers can be heard here in full effect: the pause that delivers. Labelle discovered the power pause on earlier recordings and used all hell out of it as only they could. It first occurs here after the chorus of *mocha-choca-lata-ya-ya*s: a snare smack, then a drop-out gap in the music for Patti to announce, "Creole Lady Marmalade," at first in a low, ominous stage whisper, causing you to caution whomever is near . . . *Oh hell, here she comes, get ready* . . . because over the course of the next few minutes this trick is gonna build into a funked-up nuclear frisson.

I love the moments where the band drops out and we hear the naked vocals, how Patti colors and creates her vowel shapes, the harmonic strands of all three singers weaving a clove-hitch witchery of a knot. Toussaint knew precisely where to lock out the spaces for Patti, Nona, and Sarah to fill with vocal napalm. And listen to that glorious organ intro, manhandled with sexy love. Is it Toussaint? Or could it be Art Neville? Is it a Wurli? Or a B3? I can't help but nerd out on the music here. The band on "Lady M." (and the entire LP) is made up of a nastee NOLA brass section, assorted members of Labelle's touring band, and Art Neville and the Meters (co-originators of funk alongside James Brown). The musicians all play to the sexed-up dynamics of the vocals in a circular gang bang of sound, like they've been doing it together for decades and know just what spots to hit. Toussaint's and Neville's keys and piano stylings are all over this song, and the remaining tracks on the LP have this same flavor of bayou gospel funk.

Vicki is credited as executive producer, and studio engineers Ken Laxton and Roberta Grace oversaw the recording sessions, with Toussaint checking in and signing off as the songs were completed. Apparently, the stylish Toussaint wasn't around too often during the recording sessions for *Nightbirds*, unless he was playing keys or approving sessions. His Sea-Saint Studios in the Gentilly area of New Orleans had a separate private office above the recording and control rooms, connected by an intercom. It seems Maestro didn't mind keeping people waiting, often issuing his production directives through the intercom. This funny little drama of Toussaint as deus ex machina, the sudden voice of God popping in when least expected, made for laughs, accentuating the mad fun of the party.

Labelle spent two months in the studio recording *Nightbirds*, keeping Patti away from her husband and young son, Zuri. Quite a difference from the four hours they spent recording all the vocals on *Gonna Take a Miracle*. If the music didn't calm Patti's impatience, the food surely did. To everyone's delight, sessions were catered by Toussaint's personal chef, Pots, who cooked up spicy Creole dishes and delivered nightly. You know the food had to be slammin' if Chef Patti (who would eventually write her own best-selling cookbooks) points it out in her memoirs.

When Labelle and Vicki returned home to listen to the master mixes of *Nightbirds* with fresh ears, they were gravely disappointed. Vicki tells me, "We couldn't believe it, all that work and we knew it sounded amazing, but the tracks did not come off like the music they made in the studio." A lousy mix must have felt soul crushing. Labelle would bring in another collaborator, the engineer and music-tech master Don Puluse, to remix the LP. Puluse recorded and mixed luminaries like Miles Davis, Sly and the Family Stone, Charles Mingus, and Janis Joplin; chances are you've listened to his mixes on many of your favorite discs. Puluse taught music tech at the Berklee College of Music for twenty years. He saved Labelle's record.

"Voulez-vous coucher avec moi, ce soir?" has to be

the most sexually provocative chorus in the history of hit music. A self-proclaimed anthem from the POV of a sex worker, it's a narrative the pop-consuming public had never heard before but were delighted to parrot. The song's narrative switches between the POV of a hooker and her john (or, should I say, victim). The "Joe" in question here is as helpless as a fly in the mocha milk while libertine Marmalade calls the shots, leaving the shaken man begging for "more, more, more!" Labelle snatches the plea from his chest, shakes it like a rag doll in a lion's toothy clench, and holds it aloft while our jaws drop. Scandalous as the song initially was in 1974, it remains as one of the world's most beloved pop songs. Even John Lennon felt its eargasm and can be heard playing and singing the chorus on audio captured in Paris from a rare bootleg (available on YouTube).[2]

Aside from the early blues singers, Black women didn't talk about sex in song too often. There were exceptions; Eartha Kitt, Tina Turner, and Nina Simone come to mind. And then Betty Davis arrived with "He Was a Big Freak," followed by Chaka Khan and Rufus with "You Got the Love," funkin' up the erotic. These women had had it with the racist tropes about Black women's sexuality. The demonization of Black women sprang from the hate well of slaveholders attempting to justify rape, decrying the "Jezebel" who made them do it, thus forcing the Black female erotic underground. It took a minute for Patti to come around, but Labelle ultimately refused to negate their sexual power—spoken of by Audre Lorde as a largesse beyond the sexual encounter where "every level upon which I sense also opens to the erotically satisfying experience, whether it is dancing, building a bookcase, writing a poem, examining an idea."[3]

The 1970s was the era of the feminist sex wars, battles around how women's sexuality should be presented (as opposed to embodied, in the Lordeian sense). With pornography on the rise and the loosening of sexual conventions, conflicts about what to show and how to show it were debated among second-wave feminists, with Andrea Dworkin slamming pornography on one side and sex-positive feminists Ellen Willis, Florynce "Flo" Kennedy, Audre Lorde, and the Lesbian Sex Mafia (Dorothy Allison) in contention. Labelle didn't know it at the time, but "Lady Marmalade" would further a liberating shift of perception. Labelle seduced nations into singing along to a ferocious new sexy from the Black female point of view.

The fact that most American listeners didn't understand the song's French provocation yet couldn't stop singing it became a hot marketing ploy. Sarah recalls, "On the one hand we had the nuns in Seattle marching against our lack of morals, and on the other, radio stations running French contests to see if listeners could tell them what we were saying. We first promoted the song in France, where they thought we were three French girls, and the record quickly became a hit in France, Belgium, and Spain before it hit in the US." Labelle conquered Paris, with the single in heavy rotation at the Parisian discothèque Régine's on the

Boulevard du Montparnasse. They were preparing to rock New York City with a show attendees would never forget: the "Wear Something Silver" show at the Metropolitan Opera House.

If the defining hallmark of the boomer generation in the 1970s was SEX, "Voulez-vous coucher avec moi?" was its catchphrase. Scandal! A Philly elementary school threatened to suspend their young wards for singing Marmalade's come-on through the hallways. Nuns marched in protest against the song, and a group of Black mothers from a Catholic church in Seattle purchased ads in local newspapers condemning the song and asking people to hound radio stations into banning it. CBS TV wouldn't allow Labelle to sing the French *coucher*, and they were forced to replace it with *danser* instead. Patti speaks about her annoyance that "Lady Marmalade" was such a massive hit despite so many socially conscious Labelle songs. Patti told *Rolling Stone*, "We believed in the other stuff more than 'Lady M,' the lyrical content was just more relevant. But 'Are You Lonely' could never get to be Number One."

Nona chimes in to say the controversy around "Lady Marmalade" made her laugh: "Dodging something that's real—like prostitution—is ridiculous. I just will not hide in a closet." And as for sexuality, Nona likes appealing to both men and women. "I have no preferences. I don't limit myself. I'm all sexes. I don't know what heterosexual or bisexual or a homosexual or a monosexual is. I don't understand the differences." She would echo this in an interview with fashion and music journalist Merle Ginsberg, after going solo in the early 1980s: "I don't walk around thinking 'I'm a female, I'm a rock artist.' . . . I think about music and getting across. If I don't need to define myself, I don't need for other people to do it."[4] Nona has resisted labels and branding throughout her career. She knew "Marmalade" would be a smash as well as a prelude inviting listeners in to the rest of the LP's songs and messages.

Nightbirds is a body-soakin' fusion of New Orleans funk and soul, space glam, and rock 'n' roll. The LP bring us the stomp of the gospel past morphing into a music of liberation and flight—an erotic star-sea of possibilities, where the labor pains of musical Afrofuturism howl out a new sensibility of woman. There would be no turning back.

— 9 —

MOTHERS OF REINVENTION

In 1973, Labelle and their band rocked several shows at NYC's Village Gate. For one of the shows, Nona wore a quilted white suit emblazoned with Margaret Keane figures; Sarah, a white sheath with a painted rose running up from mid-calf to breast; and Patti, a patterned top with flowing triangular sleeves, billowy knickers, and platforms. Sure, individuality was being expressed, but the group were miles away from rock star splendor. Certain fans had watched the trio go through several costume changes; from the matching chiffon frocks and T-strap heels of Bluebelle days to the Norma Kamali cowrie-shell couture on the cover of "Goin' on a Holiday."

When music onstage goes nuclear, clothes hardly matter. And yet, Afronauts need their space suits, and Labelle were about to lift off. One fan and observer in particular knew Labelle's look didn't match the heat of their biosphere. This handsome charmer approached Vicki to talk about the band's new sound, asking if they might be open to costuming. Turns out he was speaking Labellian; they needed a distinctive style to match their sound, something outrageous. Vicki confirmed how they'd love a new look but couldn't afford bespoke costumes. The fan and designer's name was Larry LeGaspi, and money needn't buy his love; he was at their service. His sartorial vision for the group helped create the iconic superstars we'd meet in their *Nightbirds* incarnation. Patti explained, "When we started I was a bit shy, but putting on those clothes let the monster out and once it was out, we were happy to go as far as he wanted. . . . Larry helped three crazy black ladies with a lot of nerve make history."[1]

LeGaspi began designing Labelle's stage wear around the time of *Pressure Cookin'*. He was gay, Puerto Rican, and subversively imaginative, all qualities granting him passage into goddess territory. He joined Labelle as couturier, immediately grasping the syncretic futurism of Labelle's new music. In a YouTube clip of Labelle performing "Lady Marmalade" on Dutch television, their outfits are mythic. Sarah appears like Athena, her bodice made of owl, pheasant, and peacock feathers. Nona is Nyx, Greek goddess of the night. Clad all in black and silver, she wears a cowl encrusted with mirrors, shoulder blades sprouting black wings, while handcuffs and a whip dangle from her belt. The effect is Afrofuturist dominatrix meets *Devil Girl from Mars*. Patti, the most physically dynamic of the three, needs to move in her outfit of flowy turquoise. An arrangement of jewel-toned partridge, marabou, and turkey feathers cascades and ripples as she waves her arms in gestures of flight: Egyptian Ma'at, meet Jane Jetson. LeGaspi worked more of the tribal with a unique trapunto-quilted African grass skirt for Patti, topped with royal headgear in silvery blue.

Another show, another costume; Sarah appearing as an Elizabethan Black Venus in an ornate silver breastplate created by LeGaspi's partner, jewelry designer Richard Ecker. The outfit sweeps up into a standing quilted collar. Below the midriff, she wears a silver hip-wrap of Egyptian draping. Sarah was giving the most body; Larry wanted her around when he was designing for her so his team could mold the clothes precisely to her shape. As Sarah said, "He would come to our rehearsals and just sit there, and the next thing you knew we'd get an extra feather or row of piping. Nobody ever thought a singer would take off her clothes and wear only a bra. That [bra] was a molding of my actual breasts. He had to make the silver on the skirt, so it actually molded to my hips. He had a strong generous spirit and mind, the way he thought about presenting his costumes with our sound."[2]

Labelle's new costumes were all about excitement and imagination, diametrically opposed to their sweet girl-group drag of bland. Makes me think of Oscar Wilde's adage: "Give [a man] a mask, and he will tell you the truth." In this case, give a woman a mask, and its truth will set her free. LeGaspi and Labelle were also reflecting the times. Outer space was part of the zeitgeist of 1960s America, with *Star Trek*, *2001: A Space Odyssey*, and Apollo 11's moon landing. The radio DJ and entertainer Jocko Henderson, known as the Ace from Outer Space and later as the grandfather of rap, played with space themes as early as the mid- to late 1950s. Henderson created tinfoil space suits and presented shows at the Apollo where he'd swoop onto the stage in a homemade rocket ship accompanied by a puff of smoke.

Space themes in music pushed to the forefront with David Bowie's "Space Oddity" released in 1969, a theme continuing into the early 1970s à la Bowie and his Spiders from Mars. Glam was a rebellion against a mainstream rock sound that had become increasingly pop and vanilla, void of sexy outrage (think Loggins and Messina, the Allman Brothers). Other musicians dealing with space themes as early as the 1960s were Jimi Hendrix, Pink Floyd, and Marc Bolan. Alice Coltrane stands out as the sole woman composing astral journeys at the time, interlacing space with the mystic. *Cosmic Music* (with husband John Coltrane), *World Galaxy*, and *Astral Meditations* are just a few LPs in a career that spanned nearly forty years. (One of my ten "desert island" discs is her *Journey in Satchidananda*.)

In 1974, the same year Labelle released *Nightbirds*, pharaoh of Afrofuturistic beginnings Sun Ra appeared in a filmed version of his philosophy called *Space Is the Place*, where Ra and his Arkestra leave their planet and arrive in Oakland, California. Ra wants to resettle African Americans on his new planet, the means of transport there being music. When Ra first arrives on Earth, he opines, "The people have no music that is in coordination with their spirits. Because of this, they're out of tune with the universe."

Nona was listening: "I felt a connection with Sun Ra through my discovery of quantum theory and quantum physics. Seeing Sun Ra and [his band] the Arkestra playing in a small club in Philadelphia in my twenties and being completely mesmerized by the music, the look, the intensity of the sound . . . I was blown away. My interest in space travel and music felt like it was on the same plane as Sun Ra's words and sounds, his animated frequencies and vibrations, which manifested in the symbolic dress he wore, the ritualized acts of prayers and repeated incantations."[3] (In February of 2020, Nona produced a show called "Nona Hendryx and the Disciples of Sun Ra in the Temple," in the Egyptian wing of the Metropolitan Museum of Art.)

Afrofuturism spins the Afrodiasporic to life in new ways by redefining the Black experience as nonlinear in space and time, circling what was and what can be, heading for the what-ifs. As Sun Ra called it, "space is the place" where institutional authorities cannot project their oppressive visions. For Labelle's costumes, LeGaspi stitched the syncretic, mixing things up in this Afrofuturist spirit. He combined medieval chain mail with silver platform space boots, Afronautic helmets and headdresses with ear-dangle jewelry of moon and stars, neckpieces, armor, and cuffs designed by Richard Ecker. Nona tells me, "Richard Ecker was really important. He worked with Larry, and together they had the Moonstone boutique together in the West Village on Hudson Street. No one ever talks about Richard, but his jewelry designs were fundamental to the costumes."[4]

LeGaspi's silver space suits confirmed Labelle as rock goddesses when they appeared on the cover of *Rolling Stone* in July 1975, the first Black vocal group to claim the territory.[5] Sarah and Nona don their space suits, with Sarah showing much skin and Nona's face bedazzled. Patti hides her body beneath a leotard, accessorized with LeGaspi silver quilting and Ecker's space earrings. (Nona's and Sarah's cone bras are clearly the prototype for Madonna's cone bras designed by Jean Paul Gaultier fifteen years later.) All three singers appear utterly astonished, as if caught in flagrante next to the headline "Sex! LABELLE: Comin' Comin' Comin' to Getcha." The inside caption to the interview by Art Harris goes way over the top, as only a gay man might (most likely Jann Wenner)—"Mmmm ounnhaaah oh God oooh it's so good, oh baby it's Labelle"—and the article keys toward gossip and the salacious, never venturing toward the genius inside the skin. (*Rolling Stone* repeated this with the Go-Go's in 1982. The band was talked into appearing in their everyday, unsexy undies by Annie Leibovitz, possibly on a prompt from *RS*. The band was not happy when they saw the bold caption to the cover photo: "Go-Go's Put Out." Dig or gaffe? Wenner again?)

LeGaspi incorporated a sewing technique first developed in thirteenth-century Sicily. From the Italian word meaning "to quilt," *trapunto* involves outlining rows of stuffing in running stitches to create three-dimensional shapes that defy the gravity of fabric's draping. LeGaspi designed belled-out skirts and stand-up collars—nouveau, winged shapes formed by hand quilting that he spent hours stitching himself. He also paid keen attention to the visual balance between the three singers, in color and shape: each singer's individuality is always reflected in LeGaspi's triadic costuming schemes. His space suits for Labelle caused a sensation; soon after the group debuted his designs, the band KISS and George Clinton's P-Funk set to chasing LeGaspi for a piece of his magic.

Lenny Kravitz is a man who understands the elements required for rock stardom. When I spoke with him about Labelle, he observed,

Everybody from James Brown, Labelle, Jimi Hendrix, Parliament-Funkadelic . . . what I love is when an artist gives you great music, musicianship, songwriting, production, and then also goes out on the stage and gives you a strong presentation. Putting all those elements together is what makes an iconic rock star. The first [Labelle] song I remember was "Lady Marmalade." It was in the streets, it was the culture, and it was the new sound. When I saw the presentation, by these beautiful Black women in avant-garde costumes, I was mesmerized. They were originators who influenced such a wide range of artists, from KISS to Miles Davis. Today we're living in a time where Afropunk is leading the way in alternative Black music, fashion, and all-inclusiveness, giving a platform for Black people to proudly wave their freak flag high. You look at this, and you can't help but

see the influence Labelle had on Afrofuturism, which is
so relevant right now.

Stage wear started getting funky to match its grooves as
early as 1969, via George Clinton, a.k.a. Dr. Funkenstein.
Clinton flexed his own brand of costuming when he first
went tribal with a full native headdress of feathers. Parlia-
ment's 1970 LP *Osmium* had Clinton and crew in full-on
Carnival gear, with members dressed as Native American,
French revolutionary, clown, and convict. Clinton might
have referenced space here and there, like on Funkadelic's
Cosmic Slop, but it was Labelle who definitely influenced
his *Mothership Connection*. (There's a clip from 1976 of
Parliament-Funkadelic performing "Cosmic Slop," where
singer Garry Shider, wearing a diaper, sings, "Space people, universal lovers . . ." from Labelle's *Nightbirds* LP.)
When Ann Powers asked George Clinton about Labelle, he
got around to them, eventually: "Alice Cooper and David
Bowie, they were doing their thing. . . . That whole period,
everybody was going for theatrical rock. So we just said,
'Let's go all the way with it. Let's do it all.' That's what we
did, and that's what they [Labelle] were doing too."[6]

Up until Labelle's theater dropped on an unsuspecting
audience in late 1974, glam rockers rocked and funkateers
funked on separate planets. With *Nightbirds*, glam and funk
became a unique pas de deux, baptized in stardust. This
was a whole new genre, and Labelle's theme of liberation
from temporal restrictions—of color, of gender, of societal

mores—continued its dance over the triptych of LPs they recorded for Epic: *Nightbirds*, *Phoenix*, and *Chameleon*. It would be their most creative period together and their last, until they reunited for the 2008 LP *Back to Now*. Although *Phoenix* and *Chameleon* continued with themes of resurrection and changing skins, it's my opinion that *Nightbirds* is Labelle's magnum opus.

Side one of *Nightbirds* begins with "Lady Marmalade" and is followed by two socially conscious scorchers penned by Nona. Busting taboos about women addressing politricks, "Somebody Somewhere" speaks to the political maelstrom of the times, Watergate, with allusions to Tricky Dick Nixon: "The writing on the wall says that he ain't right at all, he's a liar." The song also addresses the injustice of racism, and a gospel-pumped warning drives the coda: "Be prepared! He's coming back!" This isn't the Jesus of the loaves and the fishes—it's JC Superstar of Matthew 10:34, and he's waving a machete. "Somebody somewhere, must lead us homeward to the truth in our hearts, Somebody somewhere, will hear our cries for freedom if we never stop, and no more lies shall be told, no more lives shall be sold."

In "Are You Lonely?" the musicians play a nasty minor blues, drummer holding it down with a relentless quarter-note groove, the bass and piano creating all the funk in near-rhythmic unison. Toussaint's bayou-tonk piano is stellar, and the arrangement smokes. Nona, Sarah, and Patti deliver the lyrics in a mix of outrage and compassion: that sonic rage of love utterly unique to their vocal

blend. They take us on a journey past portraits of disen-
franchised people in the "city without a heart," broken by
a system of injustice and religious hypocrisy: "See the well-
dressed preacher, living like a king, hold the unwed mother,
who's afraid to scream, see the hungry children, posing for
a shot, hear their mothers tell them, that's all we've got!
Ain't that lonely?" When they get to the climax of the chorus, singers and band go off, riding waves of emotional
release from how all that injustice makes a body feel.

Why didn't Epic promote "Are You Lonely?" After such
a massive hit with "Lady Marmalade," why wouldn't they
want to follow up with another no-brainer smash? "What
Can I Do for You?" was also a potential hit, but at a tight
three minutes and eight seconds, "Are You Lonely?" presents a powerful, danceable hook with a message of empathy and the perfect timing for radio play. Stevie Wonder's
"Living for the City" reached number eight on the pop
charts and number one R&B a year before *Nightbirds*. "Are
You Lonely?" was just as musically sophisticated and politically on point. Yet unloved by Epic.

Labelle had several potential hits on their Epic LPs that
were never promoted. No excuses surface; Labelle were
the perfect act in terms of a business model, with critically
acclaimed theatrical shows and TV appearances, rock-
solid management, great songwriting and production, and
astonishing vocal talent. The record industry understands
how the protest music of the 1960s and early '70s helped
build a movement. If they'd given audiences a chance to

make up their own minds about "Are You Lonely?," the public most definitely would have loved it, putting Epic on notice; forced by audience approval to elevate the song and act, this type of cry-freedom disc might have inspired other women with major record deals to step out with their own scalding truths. The music we hear shapes our culture, and since men run the major entertainment corporations, their system of dominance must be kept intact. Rock and roll was always male dominated, and you can bet there's a think-tank sensibility in place today for those picking and choosing which songs we do *not* hear, and which women artists are promoted.

The next track on *Nightbirds*, "It Took a Long Time," is a soulful love song cowritten by Bob Crewe about finding "the one." The band plays along in delicate reverence to Patti's lead. Sarah and Nona weave a tapestry of melody around Patti in an extraordinary vocal arrangement; when they sing countermelodies to Patti's lead, the notes braid as effortlessly as fingers laced in prayer. There's a reckoning scene in the denouement of Lee Daniels's *Precious*, the film adaptation of Sapphire's *Push*, where Precious's abusive mother (played to Oscar perfection by Mo'Nique) breaks down when confronted by Precious (Gabourey Sidibe) and her social worker (Mariah Carey). Precious has found the strength to break the chain of trauma, to walk away from her mother. The scene cuts to Precious walking on a busy street filled with people, holding her young children. Within her smile shines the conviction to become the kind, loving mother she never had, to herself and to her own children. She is free. The song Daniels chose to score his heroine's journey home: Labelle's "It Took a Long Time."

Lenny Kravitz tells me Lee Daniels is a "Labelle fanatic" who grew up on the same Philly streets as Patti. Daniels is one of our bravest filmmakers, unafraid to reveal where our darkest alleys might lead in order to expose the why of it, and what it might take to heal. Like Labelle, filmmaker Daniels finds the blessedness to sing that darkness into light. Kindred will always gravitate to the beat of their own.

Lenny Kravitz also played a part in Daniels's film *Precious*. He recounts a night when Patti came over to the filmmaker's place to cook: "It was a memorable night. While Patti was cooking up a storm (you know Patti can burn), Lee started playing classic Labelle tracks on the stereo and then performed an all-out lip-synch concert. He sang every word to every song with perfection. Then the ladies started singing all of the background vocals. . . . Wow, it was one of those nights."

Next up is one of Allen Toussaint's two compositions on *Nightbirds*, "Don't Bring Me Down." The track is another funky-ass blues cut that emphasizes the snare's "and 4" eighth-note upbeat, as opposed to the typical 2 and 4 backbeat. Patti is at her sassiest here as Nona and Sarah join her to warn a brother: he better recognize, not criticize. Patti goes off at the end of the bridge, but for the most part, the song takes a breather in between the usual pyrotechnics. The groove, and the way the singers ride it, slays.

Side two starts with a call to empathic arms: "What Can I Do for You?" written by Eddie Batts and Budd Ellison, whose history with Labelle helped sculpt a song perfectly suited to their voices and sensibilities. It's a bold cry for love and empowerment through the vehicle of community. Nona, Patti, and Sarah sing most of the song in unison, with Patti occasionally stepping out to improvise. The chorus out is a give-and-take ask, a sing-along that sets fire to dance floors. Another potential smash hit—all that was needed to make it so was an edit down to three and a half minutes. Nona's Afronautic invitational "Space Children" is a funky ride into intergalactic freedom. Labelle invites us to imagine a new space where we can rethink, reassemble, and redesign our lives, free of the hard-line boundaries of identity: "Reach up even higher than your mind. One look isn't all you can see . . . and no one will be there to bring you down. So stop, take a look around space, children . . . universal lovers . . ."

Toussaint's other contribution, "All Girl Band," falls a bit flat in comparison to the other songs. Describing the hardships of musical women trying to make it in a man's world, Toussaint is noble here with a feminist message, but the song lacks the passion of the remaining set. In spite of this, Patti, Sarah, and Nona can sing about your old dog Blue and make it sound extraordinary.

The set closes with another Nona song, "You Turn Me On." Nona the writer goes there on the chorus: "I come like the pouring rain each time you call my name. . . . It's good what you're doin', what you're doin'." Sarah tells me, "Nona and Patti thought the song probably wouldn't fly, but it was the second song Allen [Toussaint] wanted to record [after 'Marmalade'] and it was a winner." Patti sings it as if her life depends on the lover Labelle are addressing/undressing. When Nona and Sarah join on those choruses . . . well, let's just say whomever they're serenading surely knows their stuff.

The visceral feelings of sex—the smells, sounds, fluids, movements—spring to life for certain artists in the heat of performance. Labelle was never ashamed of talking about the release of sexual tension they experienced onstage, where the act of singing—*howling*, as Sarah puts it— becomes orgasmic. This makes sense, since merely listening to the right type of music during peak moments of emotional arousal can release a surge of dopamine. In fact, some folks are more aroused by certain musics than by touch.

Patti told *Rolling Stone* how she feels when she performs: "It's like I'm married to a million men and women when I'm out there. And when I'm married to a person, I give all I have. It's like a climax, and when the audience does it like they did last night in Atlanta, I come. When I came out during 'Space Children,' just standing there, the way they made me feel—that's an orgasm, to see people accept you right away." Sarah went on to tell Art Harris, "I feel tears and a good hurt and a good pain. It's ritualistic, spiritual. When we recorded 'You Turn Me On,' I was howlin'. It was not just sexual, it's what life is about." Patti laughed as she recounted letting go completely, and Sarah told of informing their band members before they played that they liked "to reach orgasms onstage." She finished with the line, "I really came in Philadelphia." Nona teased an S&M theme during this interview, laughing about her whip and handcuff "props." She's not into pain, she said, but likes leather outfits, calling them "cute" and admitting she has "always had a handcuff fetish."[7]

Now for the funk. I didn't call funk by its name at the time, but I sure did dance my white prepubescent behind off to the funk of James Brown and his Famous Flames (and later the JB's) in the late 1960s right through the '70s. The Meters' "Cissy Strut," the slow-grind, sexed-up funk of Isaac Hayes (and the Bar-Kays) on *Hot Buttered Soul*, Bobby Byrd (the man behind James Brown), Dyke and the Blazers, the Headhunters, Tower of Power, Sly and the Family Stone: all masters of the funk. Some Black scholars write of funk as troubled by distinctions around genres and its proximity to the word *fuck*, as in Sylvester's "Do Ya Wanna Funk" or the Brothers Johnson's "Get the Funk Out Ma Face," two tracks that prove how funk is a groove you *must* move to. As a listening fan and an occasional singer, I'll add that a certain type of scream, an "eeeYOW!" (or its closest simile), is also part and parcel to funk in the purist, or should I say nastiest, sense of the groove . . . as in a groove so hot it makes a body holler. Props to Black scholars and authors writing extensively about funk, who speak to its cultural implications far better than I: Rickey Vincent, L. H. Stallings, and Greg Tate, among many others.

Funk was never solely a Black man's domain. Several women were recording and performing funk in the late 1960s and early '70s. Three that immediately come to mind were introduced by James Brown in succession: the mother of the brilliant singer Carleen Anderson of the Young Disciples, Vicki Anderson, with "I'm Too Tough for Mr. Big Stuff (Hot Pants)" and "The Message from the Soul Sisters"; Marva Whitney, known as "Soul Sister #1," with her early feminist pleas "Things Got to Get Better (Get Together)" and "I'm Tired, I'm Tired, I'm Tired (Things Better Change Before It's Too Late)"; and Lyn Collins, a.k.a. the "Female Preacher," with "Think (About It)." Other women bringing the funk with a sass-back at the fellas in the early 1970s: Laura Lee, Jean Knight, and Millie Jackson. One white girl among the crew, the experimental Annette Peacock, rode the funk on "Pony" while singing through a Moog synthesizer. Nasty gal Betty Davis released her first solo LP in 1973, and you couldn't get much funkier than her "Anti Love Song." Chaka Khan and Rufus hit with "Tell Me Something Good" a year after Labelle's *Nightbirds*. I could go on, but I feel secure in saying that none funked with the overall majesty and wail of Labelle on the tracks where they hit the funk hardest.

Funk is all about the groove, the emphasis usually spanking on the 1: the first beat of the measure. This defining stroke of funk is laid out in Dawn Silva's 2000 solo LP

All My Funky Friends and her 5:55 thesis, "As Long As It's on the One." Silva cites Labelle as having a strong influence on many female artists, including her group, the Brides of Funkenstein. Silva tells a story about the Mothership's origins and how George Clinton was inspired by his headline acts, New Birth, and Labelle:

> Clinton was wheeled out onstage in a coffin, and he'd
> pop out wearing nothing but a white sheet. Later he bor-
> rowed not only the theme of Labelle's ["Space Chil-
> dren"] but also the silver platform boots and the towering
> headpieces. He gave bits and pieces of their images to
> his female acts, and hired the same New York designer,
> Larry LeGaspi, to design our costumes; but in theory,
> it was just an illusion. If the Brides of Funkenstein had
> been allowed to fully develop musically by using Labelle's
> format, we too may have been as successful as Madonna
> and Lady Gaga, artists who also took full advantage of
> Labelle's departure.[8]

Nightbirds was released in September of 1974. The stage show to promote P-Funk's *Mothership Connection* didn't debut until 1976, years after Labelle's descent onto stages in space gear and their songs "Space Children," "Black Holes in the Sky," and "Cosmic Dancer." Taking funk into outer space and bringing messages home, well, Labelle's Mothership did precede Clinton's, even though he popularized the term—so who's zoomin' who? And does it matter? When the majority of men speaking to, writing about, or playing music consistently omit the innovations of women from the frame, it matters. So do Larry LeGaspi's designs for Labelle; his queer genius was nearly lost to history until now.[9] The Smithsonian National Museum of African American History and Culture has acquired the silver space suit Larry designed for Nona, and designer Rick Owens recently published the book *Legaspi* about the man he claims as mentor. Brightest of supernovas, Larry was one of too many stars lost to complications from AIDS.

I've spent a lot of time in Trinidad, and Labelle's embrace of costuming reminds me of the Afro-Caribbean tradition of Carnival, a reach back to West African music-messaging, calypso, self-adornment, and dance. French masquerade traditions, East Indian festivals, and a wild assortment of influences blend into a cultural callaloo. Video-map these traditions onto an Afrodelic funked future and you have the *Nightbirds*, *Phoenix*, and *Chameleon* incarnations of Labelle.

In Trinidad, Carnival, a.k.a. "Mas" (Masquerade), is a bacchanal of creativity, honoring imagination as well as ancestral ritual. The tradition began with enslaved Africans in Trinidad mocking their French masters, mimicking their masquerade balls in an act of rebellion. Today, preparation for Carnival extends throughout the year, culminating in two days of Dionysian, costumed revelry. Imagine if an entire citizenry were taught to embrace creativity as fundamental to living, to taking breath. And imagine, again, an entire society where artistic play is engaged in communally by CEOs and street sweepers, across lines of race, class, gender, age, and religion. To play with language, to dance, sing, paint, make music, adorn oneself, share ancestral cultures and beliefs that make the spirit soar. Everyone is active, on the move. Celebrating art as life. It's Carnival's transcen*dance* of suffering I see as parallel to the work of Labelle from *Nightbirds* on.

Nona describes this vision for the group: "Labelle was nurturing an Afrofuturistic belief, vision and reality by incorporating ideas of the future in the present while being Black; daughters of Africa and Africans who survived being sold into slavery, facing extreme hostility; fear, torture, murder, rape, brain washing, imprisonment, death, and denied the respect due a full and equal human being."[10]

With *Nightbirds*, Labelle's new gospel of freedom testified to the power of creativity unfettered, and the imagination it requires not only to heal through art but to thrive. To fly.

— 10 —

AN EPIC TRIPTYCH

Nightbird's sky is never high enough
she only touches down
just to feel her wings again
laughing, crying all the way
hear the nightbird pray.

NONA HENDRYX, "Nightbird"

In 1939, the brilliant contralto Marian Anderson was due to perform for an integrated audience at Constitution Hall in Washington, DC. The hall was controlled by the Daughters of the American Revolution, who refused to grant her permission based on a "white performers only" policy. This act of racism bounced back. The injustice served to elevate Anderson in the international arts community (Anderson was a celebrated performer on European stages). In the aftermath, First Lady Eleanor Roosevelt invited her to perform at the White House and organized a concert for her on the steps of the Lincoln Memorial on Easter Sunday, where she sang "My Country, 'Tis of Thee" to an audience of seventy-five thousand, while millions listened on the radio. In 1955, Anderson became the first Black American woman to perform at New York's Metropolitan Opera House, singing the part of Ulrike the fortune-teller in Verdi's opera *Un ballo in maschera* (A masked ball). Several African American opera singers would follow Anderson to the Met's stage: Mattiwilda Dobbs, Leontyne Price, Shirley Verrett.

It wouldn't happen until October 6, 1974, but Labelle became the first African American singing group to play the Met. Asked in her memoir to recall her most profound moment as a member of Labelle, Patti answers, "The highlight musically was when Sarah Dash, Nona Hendryx and I performed at the Metropolitan Opera House."

The hype about the Met show began as soon as *Nightbirds* was released in September of '74. Vicki Wickham designed the advertising and hype; a NYC poster campaign and ads in magazines like *After Dark* requested that the audience "Wear Something Silver" to the *Nightbirds* show on October 6, 1974. Because of their hit "Lady Marmalade" and rumors of a new, outrageous image, the show sold out immediately. Those in attendance remember it as one of New York City's most legendary nights. The Met was perfectly suited to the new show's theatrics. Wickham explains, breaking into her devilish grin, "And then, of course, once we've got the clothes [LeGaspi], it was, we can't leave it like this. What if we start flying them in? What if we start, you know, using forklifts?"[1] The what-if helped shape Labelle's Afrofuturist oeuvre and rock star ascendency.

The *Nightbirds* show required stages equipped with motorized battens so the singers could be lowered onto the stage by aerial wires. Some theaters had hydraulic elevators by which Patti, Nona, or Sarah might ascend onto the stage through a sliding trap door, and Labelle's dramatic entrances were designed according to each theater's tech specifications. Their theatricality would continue through the next two album tours, with each show featuring a unique twist. Yet none would top the party at the Met. Labelle's space-age aeronautic glamour was as theatrical and original as David Bowie's *Diamond Dogs* tour, launched in June of 1974.

In Lifetime's *Intimate Portrait* biography of Patti LaBelle, assorted celebrities recall that legendary night at the Met. Debbie Allen's face lights up as she describes the show: "I was there at the Met that night when she [Patti] came flying down from the ceiling, honey. It was incredible. It was as if we were in the presence of high royalty alien people. I remember that night, we all had to wear silver. I still have that lavender silver dress. . . . I'm telling you, everybody and their mama was there." Former Labelle road manager Ken Reynolds remembers how he "never expected to see a human being walking around the Metropolitan Opera House lobby with her body sprayed silver wearing a silver jockstrap!"

Nona recalls an audience that included a broad spectrum of "Bloomingdale's Blacks, lots of gay people, young college hippie freaks, some Spanish-speaking people, and even some old people like our parents." And this was the night Sarah Dash's family finally came around full circle in support: "My father came to the Met wearing his clerical collar. He came with my mother, and that was a big moment for me. If I were going to see my daughter to be impressed, that moment would have convinced me as well."

The sold-out venue turned away hundreds of fans, and those lucky ones with tickets strutted in silver leather chaps, silver Afros and eyelashes, hairdos festooned with tinsel. If you were there, you'd have moved among the crowd Patti affectionately called the "glitterbugs," an audience of costumed fans that included a fluidly gendered group of "nuns" in silver habits. "Some of the outfits were better than ours," Patti says. "People came with their behinds sprayed silver . . . literally their butts were hanging out but they had spray paint on their butts."

Ellis Haizlip, Nikki Giovanni, and Jackie O. moved among the crowd of LGBTQ people, Black literati, teenage Puerto Rican lovebirds, Warhol's *Interview* gang, Alvin Ailey dancers, theater folk, and art-world royalty. Jackie O. was so impressed by Labelle that night, she invited them to perform in a tribute to Josephine Baker she would sponsor there a year later.

As the Met's dramatic starburst chandeliers ascended to the ceiling, Thelma "Butterfly" McQueen stepped out in front of the curtains, introducing the show to the roaring crowd.[2] Labelle opened Act 1, "Prelude in Silver," with "Space Children," dressed in LeGaspi's Labellian Afronautica; what Jamaica Kincaid would refer to in a *Village Voice* review as "a Puerto Rican's idea of Negroes from Mars."

(Surprising, since Kincaid is from Antigua, an island that celebrates Carnival and all its eccentricities of costuming, much like Trinidad. She would later regret writing the bad review.) The crowd lost their minds to every song and its accompanying spectacle. Luther Vandross remarked, "Oh! It was hysteria!"[3]

"Space children, universal lovers, space children. Are there any others? You better take a look if you're in doubt!" Contained in that last line is a provocation to the audience to see each other—the audience here just as imaginatively dressed as the supersonic performers onstage. The music and the costumes showcased in the Met's dramatic setting made for an unforgettable moment. Labelle closed Act 1 in the loving sonic embrace of the Mt. Vernon Gospel Chorus, a Black youth choir singing Nona's inspirational lyrics: "I believe that I've finally made it home, and I believe that with me there's nothing wrong. . . . I believe their thoughts are inane, and I'm all right, while this whole political world has gone insane."

Act 2 of the show opened with Sarah encased in black feathers, a Black swan standing at the top of a staircase. As she turned toward the audience, she began to sing an intro missing from the recording: "Nightbird fly by the light of the moon . . . she's flying high and all alone." Nona appeared dressed in a white space suit, breasts and crotch studded in silver, and a three-foot-high crown of white feathers. The Aztec space-goddess wear continued—cue spotlight—as a glowing bird descended from on high, suspended from rings and wires, wings spread to reveal a twenty-foot train of feathers. Patti hits the stage, drops the feathered cloak to reveal a copper quilted space suit beneath. She starts to sing. The crowd jumps to their feet, wailing.

"Lady Marmalade" created bedlam, and Labelle knew just how to orchestrate the mood, bringing it down to a hush for a dramatized rendition of "Can I Speak to You Before You Go to Hollywood?" The show concluded with Patti, Sarah, Nona, and band members dancing through the aisles on the encore of "What Can I Do for You?," grabbing hands, hugging, playing percussion instruments, the ecstatic audience dancing along, shaking tambourines and maracas in a carnival of boundary-busting celebration. The following day, the papers sang holy praise, and the city was besieged by talk of the show. Labelle had conquered New York.

Labelle toured France, England, the Netherlands, Belgium, Spain, and the United States with their *Nightbirds* show. In March of 1975, they played the Santa Monica Civic Auditorium, where old friend Reggie Dwight—Elton John—introduced them to a crowd of celebrities, joining them for an encore parade through the audience. "Lady Marmalade" and *Nightbirds* rocketed Labelle into superstardom. After criminally underselling "Are You Lonely?," Epic released "What Can I Do for You?" as a follow-up. Ubiquitous on dance floors in 1975, the track went to number seven on the dance chart, but Epic failed to do a radio-friendly edit, and the song didn't chart pop or R&B. Epic wanted Labelle back in the studio ASAP for a follow-up LP and single. Disappointed about "Lady M." being the only successful single off the LP, Labelle returned to Allen Toussaint's studio in the late spring of 1975 to try and replicate the previous magic of *Nightbirds*.

I liken the Vedic trinity of creativity, sustainment, and destruction as metaphor to Labelle's Epic trilogy of *Nightbirds*, *Phoenix*, and *Chameleon*. If every act of creation is also an act of destruction, *Chameleon* would represent the full cycle of this triadic—as it ends, to begin again. The cover of *Phoenix* features all three singers with heads lifted skyward, eyes closed, white gowns (choir gowns as wings) blurred in upward motion, in a sustainment of flight.

When asked if she considers herself a phoenix, Nona tells me, "Yes, I think so. I constantly keep rising from some incarnation of myself into another one." On *Phoenix*, the story of the "Nightbird" is reborn with the continuing emergence of Nona's more theatrical rock writing. The opening track, "Phoenix (The Amazing Flight of a Lone Star)," offers a continuance of past lyrical themes: flight, rebirth, erotica, space, and transcendence. The lone star in the parenthetical part of the title is the phoenix rising, Lady M. transformed into *griotte*: "In a red dress, she dances the blues, races the dawn, to bring us the news . . . (come on, sing the news)." In this mini opera, Patti plays phoenix to Sarah and Nona's Greek chorus. The song conjures the image of a "fallen" woman scorned, of generations of women waiting in shadows, hiding dreams "in old mason jars" (a nod to Vicki's childhood; glass jars shuddering to the beat of German bombs), and finally redeemed by the grace of flight.

At the song's end, the band creates a space for the singers to fill with mythic sweetness: the "string" of a held note, an A#6 (in the third octave above middle C) at the top, guiding the ascension. Labelle show off their mastery of musical rests here, the negative spaces becoming a pregnant void where one engages in a type of meta-listening, waiting for Patti to bring it home. She does just that as prelude to the band kicking into double time.

Swapping out the funk grooves of *Nightbirds* for edgier rock seasonings, many of the songs on *Phoenix* feature more complex structures, pauses, and dropouts lengthening to punch each story's drama. Aside from a few tracks, the funkiness of the musical arrangements heard on *Nightbirds* is lacking here, and the idea of playing the songs with rock inflections casts some of the tracks as a bit plodding. Funk maestro Toussaint might not have felt as inspired about the rock influence of these songs. Add to this Patti's vocals here . . . she felt torn over leaving son Zuri and husband Armstead to record another LP, which would ultimately lead to another tour and too much time away from home. And she wanted to sing her ballads. But the group had flown over the rainbow, reborn as an entity beyond Patti's musical needs. A close listen to *Phoenix* indicates a feeling of unease . . . a slight pallor. As if Patti did not have the total conviction she typically brought to a lyric. Nevertheless, there are gems on the LP, and the title track, "Phoenix (The Amazing Flight of a Lone Star)," is a masterpiece.

Many of the songs, such as "Cosmic Dancer" and "Black Holes in the Sky," have Nona (the writer) continuing with the intergalactic, her husky, subliminal harmonic anchoring Sarah, whose voice brings the sweet wild of a space-femme howl. The musical arrangement on "Black Holes" doesn't do justice to the lyric and melody and the atmosphere the song provokes. I can imagine how a different producer might have arranged this track. Patti sounds like she's merely going through the motions, not really feeling the message: "Behold, black holes in the sky. I'm told a shining star lives inside." Nona's and Sarah's vocals are more prominent in the arrangements and the mix on many of the songs. In "Slow Burn," the lyric talks about a community's inability to face pain, personally and collectively. They sing in unison, "We live on the doorstep of pleasure, we bury our martyrs in vain. We must raise ourselves up much higher, to renege is to live it again." The song's warning: when you back out of facing the wound, you'll only have to experience its pain again down the road. Patti is giving effortless vocal pyrotechnica here, but I can't help but feel her heart was back home in Philly.

Toussaint might have phoned in most of the production on *Phoenix*, but we definitely hear his swampy influence on "Take the Night Off" and its *Streetcar Named Desire* atmosphere—a humid and bluesy slow drag. Patti throws sass while Nona and Sarah do a slippery chorus resolving with a punched "Take it!" Maestro stomps all funky again for "Messin' with My Mind," a sizzling dance track with distinctive NOLA horn parts working off vocals arranged in slick counterpoints of dynamic hits and phrasing. Had someone from Epic fought for Labelle and hired a DJ to excise sixty seconds for a seven-inch edit, it could have been a Top 10 hit.

All three women of Labelle have spoken about their lack of hits being due to radio's rules around genre and Labelle's music resisting the boxes of straight-up R&B or rock. Yet I believe plenty of Labelle tracks were "radio friendly."

Perhaps some of the "unfriendliness" was due to male record execs and radio jocks being intimidated by such strong erotic vocal and lyrical power from women on wax. A case in contrast: the Isley Brothers scored a number four pop hit and a number one R&B hit with "Fight the Power" in 1975, in the same year and on the same record label as Labelle's *Phoenix*. The track is a hard-hitting funk slice with passionate vocals speaking live and direct to the power. The guitarist Ernie Isley has talked in interviews about how the Isleys resisted being confined to a category and how they were influenced by Jimi Hendrix (a member of the Isleys for a brief time and, coincidentally, a third cousin of Nona's). Jimi put *wah-wah* on the map with "Voodoo Chile." Hardly your garden variety R&B musician, Hendrix—his rock famously copulating with funk—makes a person wonder, *Where do the coordinates separate? And why should they?* Hendrix and the Isleys flipped the bird at musical apartheid and succeeded on the charts. Why did "Fight the Power," with its message about having to fight against a perpetual beatdown by "bullshit" (and yes, Ronald Isley *goes there*), shoot to the top of the charts but not "Messin' with My Mind"? A song calling out a partner's shoddy treatment, even if it's analogous to a much bigger, nastier mess, was less controversial than the Isley Brothers track. With Patti singing, "I'm spent, you win, I'm gonna give you up for Lent!" (great line) plus a killer hook, "If you keep it up, gonna give you up!" riding a formidable beat, who wouldn't wanna shake it in agreement?

The reason that "airplay is not fair play" has more to do with the record company's politically shaped convictions and cash layout. When a corporate record company drops the ball on an act, radio's lack of ardor is blamed, but I cry bullshit along with the Isleys. Labelle was robbed of the hit singles they deserved because they were strong Black women who sang aggressively, a self-contained group unwilling to kowtow to insecure white male notions of how women should behave. That is, if they expected to win the support of Daddy Warbucks. Despite their talent for creating stellar tracks with strong messages people genuinely wanted to hear, Labelle would continue to slam up against music industry bias.

The tension bubbling within the group was in part due to the industry's negligence. Nona's ascendance as a songwriter and a creator of rock theater was also a bit unsettling. Labelle's direction was beginning to feel at odds with

Patti's desire to sing more traditional R&B ballads, where she felt most comfortable vocally and emotionally. Patti was in a vulnerable place, and this might have been due to her being a wife and new mother. Sarah must have been acutely aware of all the tensions. She remained the middle presence, Ms. Switzerland calming the waters.

The *Phoenix* LP reached number ten on the R&B album chart and number forty-four pop, despite its lack of high-charting singles. Labelle toured to support the LP in the fall of 1975, incorporating many of the same theatrics of previous shows with thematic twists. They continued to gather new disciples. The hottest tracks from the Epic trilogy, "Lady Marmalade," "What Can I Do for You?," and "Messin' with My Mind," were ubiquitous on dance floors, especially at the pre–Studio 54 gay spots in NYC: Le Jardin, the Loft, and 12 West. Patti honored her commitment to promote, but the demands of touring exacerbated the ongoing absences from her family. Patti brought along a suitcase full of cooking gear when touring—pots and pans, a hot plate, spices—and would prepare meals for the band. She prided herself on being the mama of the entourage, and the nurturance was appreciated; being on the road isn't as glam as people might think. While touring in October of 1976, Patti was hit with a crisis: her sister Vivian passed away from lung cancer. The gravitational pull of family and Philly would continue to tug at Patti's heart.

Chameleon was the third and final LP of Labelle's deal with Epic. A changeling creature whose bones glow through its skin, the color-shifting chameleon feeds into Labellian themes of renewal and transformation, the "skin diving" Nona Hendryx would continue to explore in her solo career. David Rubinson stepped into the producer's seat for *Chameleon* after coming off the successful LP *Steppin'* by the Pointer Sisters.

This LP is astonishing. The opening cut, "Get You Somebody New," is a tour de force of funk with its searing demand for freedom. When I meet someone who knows how to move with me on a dance floor to this jam, I may even fall in love again. Carmine Rojas's slinky, funked bass sets up the groove, and you never want that groove to end. Seventies-style *wah-wah* scratch guitar (Wah Wah Watson, Eddie Martinez), Tower of Power horns, and serious drum play funk the percussion building the heat, and the vocals are gospel-driven, call-and-response gunpowder. In unison they sing, "I can't stand it!" and the three faces of Eve's libido respond: Patti with "when you call my name," Nona all sexy heat with "drive me insane," and Sarah wailing the high climax with "heart's desire!" Back to the three together: "hurts like fire!" When they commence the *unh-unh*s in the vamp out, playing off that devilish funk and countering the jazzy horn stabs and runs, it's naah-steee: straight-up sex on wax. Radio would never play anything as volcanically erotic from women as this slice of sweat. If you're not compelled to move your body to this track, call the embalmer. Donna Summer's "Love to Love You Baby" is baby's bassinet time in comparison.

The singing on *Chameleon* feels more passionate and authentic, the musical arrangements and mixes far superior to most of the tracks on *Phoenix*. Patti is feeling it on this LP, and the Labellian roar, as well as the gut instincts of where to come down sweet and rise up wild, are here in full effect. Ballads such as "Come into My Life" and "Isn't It a Shame" are as smooth and as righteous as gospel lullabies turned up to eleven. "Who's Watching the Watcher?" is a song about political apathy, piano ringing and beat pumping in the rock style of an Elton John song, but with that glorious gospel wail.

The title song, "Chameleon," is an invitational stroll—"Come with me if you believe"—and toward the end morphs into an interstitial spell where delays and repetitions turn into a trippy amniotic swirl, percussion building as they sing, "If you believe in the magical world . . ." The band drops down to percussion and keyboard glissandos as they chant a mantra bathed in spooky delay. The spell builds, whirls, and then something extraordinary happens. A rock guitar lead, Jesus Christ Superstar–style, is born from this womb of sound, a descending riff suddenly filling out as the band joins for chords reversing direction, climbing upward . . . and BAM, the group breaks into the salsa funk sweat of "Gypsy Moths." This incredible transition is rock opera territory. "Let the fire be your goal, and you can dance. Let the music in your soul so you can dance." The gypsy moths salsa under the volcano, inviting us to the immortal circle dance of creation and destruction.

Labelle is in peak form here, with Nona stepping front and direct all over this record. She takes the lead on her composition "A Man in a Trenchcoat (Voodoo)," a mystery about an encounter with a shape-shifter on a dark night in New Orleans. In the song's outro, Nona goes off with whispered conjurings reminiscent of Patti Smith's hallucinatory poetics on the mic. But Nona wasn't happy with the mix of *Chameleon* or with David Rubinson's production. She and Sarah would have preferred Patti not sing "Isn't It a Shame," but Patti pursued Rubinson about the track and won. Tensions were building; Nona wanted to pull the act in a more theatrical direction, with Sarah happy to join that ride, while Patti longed to sing ballads and spend more time with her family. Patti had suggested doing a solo LP as a side project but was shot down by the others.

Chameleon concludes with a ballad, "Going Down Makes Me Shiver." Lezbionic? Screw the identity tags: a VIP wristband is guaranteed to anyone singing this song at the gates of the pink. Talk about a double entendre. Certainly no stranger to gay culture, Patti doesn't back away from a testimony that reads as much about higher love as it does the act of kneeling to Eros. Pair this with "You Turn Me On" from *Nightbirds*, and sexy doesn't come much stronger. At the end of this closing track, Patti whispers as if she's done in, with Nona and Sarah singing "going, going." Their voices repeat and fade into a final groove.

In the *Rolling Stone* cover story, a young woman at Labelle's Atlanta show says, "Lesbians love Labelle." For dykes of my generation, Labelle were our David Bowie, the first women performers to present an erotic image far beyond the dictates of heteronormativity. Comparing the queer Black performance artist Kevin Aviance to Labelle, José Esteban Muñoz posits how Labelle "reconstructs blackness as a mysterious Lost-in-Space aesthetic."[4] Patti's been queer friendly since the Chitlin' Circuit days (yes, there was a *gay* side of the circuit), referring to Labelle's LGBTQ audience as her "children." Labelle's gay male audience is as fanatical as Judy Garland's; the flamboyance of Labelle's costumes, the dramatic song-stories, the eroticism and fluid sexuality, not to mention the brilliant singing were, and still are, queer lures for the boomers, and hopefully for the generations yet to discover them.

Chameleon went to number ninety-four on the pop chart and number twenty-one R&B. "Get You Somebody New" was released as a single with weak chart results, and "Isn't It a Shame" reached number eighteen on R&B. All very modest successes, but not enough to stoke promo heft from the record company. Labelle toured *Chameleon* in the summer of 1976. There's a clip of them on *Don Kirshner's Rock Concert* in 1976, a must-see, with Labelle wearing outfits designed by Norma Kamali: embroidered mud-cloth tunics and headdresses, vests, bodices, and skirts made of cowrie shells and macramé. African *griotte* queens from outer space. The chic skew on primal goddess-wear matched the plan moving forward: the next LP would be called *Shaman*. The band and Vicki were planning a musical that

Nona was creating as a Broadway event, with a tour of the theater circuit.

Patti described it this way: "The show's going to be called *Nile Women*. We're going to give it to schools for kids to do, colleges, for anybody to do. And we can take it out on the road whenever we want. It's just like a Broadway play, like *Guys and Dolls*."

Nile Women never came to be. Labelle toured several cities with *Chameleon* in 1976 and decided to call it quits after a show in Baltimore. Tensions had escalated to the point of no return. Patti was anxious and homesick, longing to get back to family and the ballads she loved. Sarah was stuck in the middle, trying to hold down the fort while imagining what might be next for her, personally and professionally. Nona was surfing new galaxies, coming into her own singular artistry, dreaming up worlds. As long as Labelle continued touring, Patti's home, husband, and the young son growing up without her would remain a sideline. This did not sit well with Patti. Shooting holes into a boat already filling with uneasy waters, Epic failed once again on several should-have-been hits from *Chameleon*.

Nona's growing prominence as the architect of future galaxies, her far-reaching ambitions for the group, and her taking over the lead vocal duties on "A Man in a Trenchcoat" might have shaken Patti. Nona and Sarah were stepping out for more solo vocal passages on each subsequent LP, and the vision for the band going forward was clearly about giving their two voices more solo time and love. Patti

might have felt the place of dominance she'd held so effortlessly for fifteen years was being eroded by the people she
was closest to, a difficult dynamic to grapple with. And
of course, there was the vexatious rock and roll lifestyle
women rock stars sometimes indulge in as voraciously as
their brothers. Nona and Sarah were single, ultra-hot rock
stars. One might correctly imagine that groupies were not
in short supply. Patti was a beauty and had her own share of
fans, but she didn't roll that way, drawing a hard line when
it came to certain rock star excesses, which placed her as the
outsider. When a band is as tight as Labelle had been for all
those years, it's nigh impossible to hide what you feel. The
cracks began to show onstage.

The YouTube clip of *Don Kirshner's Rock Concert* in 1976
that I mentioned earlier will tell you everything you need to
know about how brilliant Labelle were at this point in their
career. Labelle and their band are combustible, their heat
setting the stage and the audience on fire. One must forgive
if the speed of the group on "Are You Lonely?" indicates
they might have been snowcappin' backstage, because the
performance and playing are supersonic. Bathed in sweat,
Patti goes *off* at the end of the song, singing the audience onto their feet. There's a lot of play between Patti
and Sarah, hand-holding and the like, but throughout the
show, Patti and Nona avoid any physical touch. They dance
around each other and deliberately do not meet outside
the parameters of their vocal harmonies. Patti had always
resisted change, but this time she wouldn't be talked out of

what everyone knew to be inevitable. Vicki tells me Patti was the one to call the conclusion: "It's time we stop . . . let's end while we're friends."

Most destructive of flying insects, gypsy moths strip trees of their foliage to expose the branches, leaving just enough for the tree to survive and regenerate. Curiously, these moths avoid the flowering dogwood, its four blood-tinged petals symbolic of Christ's crucifixion. Did Labelle feel the prescience of their song "Gypsy Moths"? Labelle had created a new Black womanhood of song, the sweep of three souls in flight demanding the destruction of held ideas. They had reached an apogee. It was time to break the triad into separate resurrections.

— 11 —

APOTHEOSIS:
WOMEN WHO FLY

In 1977, Patti and Nona signed solo recording deals with Epic. When Don Kirshner heard that Sarah was available he jumped, signing her to his label (ironically, a subsidiary of CBS, Epic's parent company). Vicki remained with Nona and Sarah as manager, and Patti's husband, Armstead, took over management duties for Patti.

Initially, Patti felt insecure without Nona and Sarah. They had experienced so much since first coming together as teenagers. Patti often talks about feeling unmoored without them and anxious about singing solo, but Epic didn't give her time to adjust. They wanted Patti in the studio ASAP. She returned to David Rubinson, the producer of *Chameleon*, for her first solo effort, the self-titled *Patti LaBelle*. Released in early 1977, the album reveals Patti in great form, with a more conservative approach to the music—nothing too edgy or wild. Her cover of "Funky Music," previously set to blazes by Edwin Starr and the Temptations, is more of an after-dinner funk digestif. Most tracks on the LP are nicely arranged R&B, including the ballads Patti loves to sing. The killer of this set is "You Are My Friend," its vocal play and dropouts toward the end, chill inducing.

Patti's first solo LP marks the beginning of an illustrious solo recording career. As of this writing she has released over sixteen LPs, many selling platinum and gold. "On My Own," her duet with Michael McDonald, went to number one on the pop charts, and other songs, such as "New Attitude" and "If Only You Knew," would cross over from the R&B charts to pop success. "If You Asked Me To" is pure R&B gorgeousity. She's covered a few songs written by Nona too; Patti realizes what a perfect fit Nona's writing always was for her voice, returning to the source. "Release Yourself" features Patti reuniting with Sarah and Nona on Patti's 1991 LP *Burnin'*. Also an actress, she has appeared in films and on several TV series, most recently as the recurring character Christine Brown on Lee Daniels's series *Star*. In late 2010 she played king of Afrobeat Fela Kuti's mother in the musical *Fela!* on Broadway. She's published several cookbooks (I can testify that her spicy dirty rice in *Recipes for the Good Life* is sublime), and her legendary sweet potato pies fly off the shelves at Walmart. Patti's memoir, *Don't Block the Blessings*, was published in 1996 and is a must read for fans of Patti *and* of Labelle.

Two Patti solo tracks pop for me personally. I fell in love to the ballad "If You Asked Me To," and the funked napalm of "All Right Now" from 1992 helped me dance my way through a rough breakup. The latter song is a celebratory exhale of finally getting over someone, set to a nasty beat. Patti's voice is nothing less than epic. She's an instinctual performer: when she's feeling it most, she turns full-on acrobat, continuing to drop, kick, and roll while trilling a note that leaps octaves.

Burnin' won Patti her first Grammy. Aside from dozens of Lifetime Achievement and Image Awards, she has five gold albums, two platinum, and no intention of calming her musical spirit down anytime soon. She danced to "In Da Club" on *Dancing with the Stars* in 2015. She told the *Guardian*, "They call me OG. A lot of my band call me that—I am the original gangsta."[1]

As of this writing, Patti's sweet potato pie success has her expanding into a soul food line for Walmart, where you can pick up a frozen version of her popular "Over the Rainbow" mac and cheese. She has continued to love her drag—a far more played-down version than Labelle's, except for her crown. Through all her years of performance, Patti has sported hairdos as elaborate as Marie Antoinette's.

Although Patti's solo success is due to a more mainstream R&B repertoire, she hasn't lost her edge yet. Fox's reality show *The Masked Singer* asks judges to guess the identity of a singer hiding inside a costume and mask. The singer's voice is also disguised by filters and processing. Patti played the "Flower" on season 2. About her surrealist turn on the show, she says, "I've been in this business for 60 years, I'm 75 years young, and I've never done anything so hard and so hot and so controlled. . . . This was challenging, the most challenging thing I've ever done, in my life."[2] The original surrealists would have approved; her flower costume was as beautiful and magnificently surreal as a Cocteau film, proving she isn't as conservative as folks might think.

Ever the maverick of the group, Nona launched her solo career with a self-titled LP for Epic in 1977. She appears on the cover, a tough street girl in black jeans and a tight Natural, picking a fingernail with the tip of a bowie knife—the 1977 Nona 2.0 emerging as a major player in the dystopian world of downtown NYC in the late 1970s. The city President Ford decreed should "drop dead" rebelled, flipping Ford the bird as gangs of sound and art renegades took possession of Manhattan, from the federally damned Bowery to the Bronx. Rap and hip-hop, no wave and neo-jazz, punk, funk, disco, and house music transformed the urban hell-space into a utopia of ecstatic celebration where gays, Latinxs, Blacks, white punks, nerdy art students, and vampiric dilettantes swapped cultural beats, spit, and poetry.

On Nona's song "Leaving Here Today" from her 1977 LP, she continues to invite listeners to shake the fetters off their imaginations: "Sail across an ocean dry, go where spaceships cannot fly. Do you know where this could lead? Would you like to come with me?" Declining to promote this edgy, hard-rocking LP—Nona clearly didn't fit the Black female singer paradigm or genre cage—the narrow-minded execs at Epic dropped her, but her live gigs (at least the ones I attended) were always packed. She continued writing songs for her next solo outing while contributing backing vocals on tracks by too many major artists to mention. Brian Eno and Talking Heads sought her out for their Afro-pop influenced LPs *Remain in Light* and *Speaking in Tongues*. In his memoir *Remain In Love*, Talking Heads and Tom Tom Club drummer Chris Franz talks about Nona: "The great Nona Hendryx added formidable multi-layered background vocals."[3] Hear her in the blend on "Born under Punches" and "The Great Curve," and on "Slippery People" from *Speaking in Tongues*.

Nona has a voluminous discography, so for the sake of brevity I'll concentrate on the highlights. Her lead vocal on Material's "Bustin' Out" led to a number one dance hit. Bill Laswell and the Material music posse coproduced *Nona* in 1983, on her first release for RCA. Two of her most stellar tracks, "Transformation" and "Keep It Confidential," appear on this disc. She's in prime voice and musical company: Nile Rodgers, Sly Dunbar, Ronny Drayton, Bernie Worrell, Kashif, Michael Beinhorn, Olu Dara, Raymond Jones (pianist for Chic), Laswell himself, and Jamaaladeen Tacuma. Every tune is a potential hit, from eighties dance–influenced slices such as "B-Boys" and "Run for Cover" to the reggae groove (thank you, Sly Dunbar) of "Steady Action." "Living on the Border" is just as politically relevant today as it was in 1983: "I am free inside my head, not because some paper said." Nona adds a gospel harmonic to punctuate her core theme of flying free from the boxed boundaries of identity. She's supported by exceptional vocal company: Dolette McDonald, Michelle Cobbs, and B. J. Nelson, three magnificent singers whose voices have graced many a hit record over three decades of music and counting.

Nona writes the majority of the songs on the 1983 disc, aside from "Keep It Confidential," cowritten by Jeff Kent and songwriters Ellie Greenwich and Ellen Foley. "Keep It Confidential" is easily construed as a queer plea for discretion. And yet the song flies universal when it centers on the masks we all wear, subterfuge for inner lives that do not gel with the world we walk through—and the longing beneath our masks for the "other," the one we ache to walk beside.

Released in 1983, "Transformation" had the queer community from first spin: "Rust to dust, us to them. Change your mind, change your skin. Life to death, weak to strength. Cash a check, change your sex." Nona appeared on an episode of *The L Word*, performing the song as a duet with Foxy Brown—Pam Grier—and the feminist rock group Betty. "Design for Living" was written for the LP that would have followed *Chameleon* had Labelle not dissolved. Nona brought in a superwoman posse of musicians: Tina Weymouth of Tom Tom Club and Talking Heads on bass, Laurie Anderson on violin, Valerie Simpson of Ashford and Simpson on piano, Gina Schock of the Go-Go's on drums, Nancy Wilson of Heart on guitar, and Nona's former bandmate Patti LaBelle, with Carol Steel on percussion

(Carol played the astonishing percussion on Steve Winwood's "Higher Love").

Several Nona tracks were staples in New York City's dance-club scene. "I Sweat (Going through the Motions)," with its lyric "They say do it like this, do it like that, if you want the money," showcased prime Nona: she who will never be commodified. A song Prince wrote for her under the pseudonym Joey Coco, "Baby Go-Go" features Mavis Staples and the Purple One on backing vox. "If Looks Could Kill" is a favorite, and "Why Should I Cry" was her highest-charting hit, at number five on the R&B chart.

Released in 1985 on the LP *The Heat*, Nona's powerful love anthem "I Need Love" was another home run in need of promotion that never came. The song can easily be interpreted as a rebuttal to her old pals the Rolling Stones and the cock-rocking, sexist strut of "Some Girls" off the album of the same name, critically hailed as the Stones' glorious return to form. Now, I adore the Stones, always have, and as a young butch dyke in the early 1970s, I imagined that singing "Under My Thumb" made me desirable, because don't all women love a bad boy? Jagger was a role model for my tragically uninformed romantic teenage psyche. And the LP *Some Girls* has a classic slice, "Miss You," that steals your heart while moving your behind. But on the album's title track, the Stones throw down creepy racist tropes (Jezebel and Shanghai Lil). It's all pecuniary poontang talk destined to piss off even the least politically correct among us.

Released seven years after the Stones' "Some Girls," Nona's "I Need Love" tells us who "some girls" truly are: "Some girls come from the best of homes. Some girls don't know their right from wrong. Some girls come from a dusty road, where life is hard and it's a heavy load." RCA didn't promote "I Need Love," and the gatekeepers (or homophobes) at MTV refused to run the video because it featured a panoply of sexualities, *Quel scandale!* Helmut Newton—styled women dressed in tuxedos, eighties-coiffed club kids, Ladyboys, a dominatrix: a sexual bouquet of colors and genders pass one another in the night, through hotel hallways and subway stations. Nona can have any one of them. (Five years later, Madonna would take the same video concept and push it over the brink for "Justify My Love.") What do some girls really want? Nona's lyrical strut toward a higher love is the truth Mick degraded: "I want someone to help me make it through the night. I need love, love will get me through the night." This was a hit song, no less of a perfect pop construction than Bonnie Tyler's "Total Eclipse of the Heart," a fitting aphorism for the absence of "I Need Love" on any music chart or radio playlist. And the Rolling Stones' *Some Girls*? Of course, it's the Stones: the LP went to number one. And so it goes when it comes to fiercely singular, independent women artists, no matter how many potential hits they produce. Thankfully the Stones had the decency to not promote "Some Girls" as a single.

Nona's no-wave experimental rock band Zero Cool

was a little Contortions, a bit Defunkt, and a whole lotta noise guitar, the kind of electrified, deconstructed funk-rock that helped make the late-1970s and early-1980s New York music scene so exciting. She was an artist member of the Black Rock Coalition (BRC), founded by Vernon Reid (Living Colour), author Greg Tate, DK Dyson (the singer of I and Eye), and producer Konda Mason. The BRC formed in 1985 to advocate against musical apartheid at a time when Black rock musicians were locked out of key venues that supported punk and rock of a paler persuasion. Nona produced an album for the punk-funky band the Bush Tetras, and in typical Nona fashion, she brought in Darlene Love to sing backing vocals. Says Pat Place, guitarist in the Contortions and the Bush Tetras, "Nona was very experimental with her own music at the time, and with us. Her energy was amazing. She'd show up at our session after leaving a kick-boxing class. She was always on the go."[4]

When Labelle and Vicki Wickham's professional and personal friendship began, Nona felt the encouragement to defy societal and musical norms in her songwriting. She has never released an LP without at least one song addressing social issues. Patti and Sarah were also profoundly affected by Vicki's influence, but it was Nona who took up the mantle of group visionary, thus shaping the flight path for the band. Nona continues to slip skins: revolutionary art rocker, new-wave goddess, skin diver, Mama Funk—sometimes all characters at once in the syncretic spirit of

Afrofuturism. Nona is anomaly and contradiction, skin diving through genres, hues, and genders, always true to her chameleon nature. In a 1975 interview, she talks about not knowing what labels like "homosexual," "monosexual," or "bisexual" really mean. From her RCA press kit: "I don't think of myself as female, I don't think of myself as a black female, and I don't think of myself as a rock artist." This is Nona maintaining her artistic integrity while throwing down a declaration of independence from the record industry.

Nona has always possessed the goods: voice, beauty, sex appeal and style, visionary songwriting chops, stage moves, and management. All in, she's the complete package necessary to become a bona fide rock superstar—and she is that, regardless of industry ignorance. Despite her lack of record company support, critics knew Nona as an innovator worthy of attention; her solo LPs garnered reviews in the *New York Times*, *Ebony*, *Creem*, *Rolling Stone*, *NME*, and *Melody Maker*. Peter Gabriel brought her on as his opening act in 1977, as did David Bowie in 1987.

Nona had it all, and still does. Did she sacrifice über-stardom by sticking to her ideals and not playing the game? Probably. I imagine she prefers it this way. No brand or genre can ever capture the sum of all that an artist is, but try and tell that to a record executive. The social engineering of music chooses whom it will transform into an icon very carefully, especially when it comes to women. In this current state of surveillance and social media toxicity, male motives about women in the entertainment industry are exposing themselves like a perp convention in a park. When men stop trying to control and objectify women, when they cease being terrified of our agency and our sexuality and finally realize their own minds have been confiscated to do the bidding of a very few autocrats at the top, we will once again hear music that truly matters. A community of sound and vision strong enough to heal millions awaits.

Nona continues to create fascinating work, most recently in multimedia performance pieces with artist Carrie Mae Weems and as an ambassador for artistry in education at Berklee. If you're looking for subversive avant-garde, listen to Nona channeling Don Van Vliet on *The World of Captain Beefheart*, the LP she recorded with Beefheart guitarist Gary Lucas: it's a set guaranteed to fire neural hormones into a wicked blaze. At Berklee, Nona works with students melding music, science, and technology into interactive audio clothing. A signature piece created by Benoît Maubrey, the "audio tutu" (a plexiglass skirt with built-in speakers), combines an audio corset/bodysuit and W.A.V.E. glove, each piece capable of triggering sounds, lights, and moving images. Nona becomes an untethered transhuman, a sci-fi machine melding flesh and tech, sound and vision. She consistently advocates for women in music as performers and creators through concerts and events, also encouraging women to study and pursue work in technology—especially women of color, whose numbers are nearly invisible in music tech and engineering.

Godmother of Sonic Afrofuturism, Nona was the artistic director of *The Cosmic Synthesis of Sun Ra and Afrofuturism*, taking place in the Egyptian wing of the Metropolitan Museum of Art. The lead performer in a series of events, she spoke about the series with Taylor Hosking for the *Observer*: "We want to show how the symbolism and imagery, sounds, and rhythms that are African in nature change in different cultures over time. Afrofuturism, Egyptian futurism and indigenous futurism are the energies that are coming together. . . . There's a need for an expression and people tend to coalesce around something they identify with. People are seeking answers and seeking a place to belong, to identify with, and possibly heal some of the harm that has been done over the centuries."[5] Her vision—on point to the work Labelle had been doing all along.

Sarah Dash released a self-titled album in 1978 and immediately scored a hit in the club scene with "Sinner Man," followed by another dance track, "(Come and Take This) Candy from Your Baby." During her tenure on Don Kirshner's label, the songs she was given to sing were not exceptional, and she didn't have much chart success. Her live-track dates (where an artist sings to a backing track that's been stripped of the lead vocal) were always packed, and the disco track "Oo-La-La, Too Soon," which was licensed for a Sasson Jeans commercial, was a nice boon. After Sarah's commitment to Kirshner expired, she worked with Megatone Records in San Francisco, releasing "Lucky Tonight," with backing vocals by Sylvester.

The track reached number five on the dance charts, due in part to its production by Patrick Cowley, Sylvester's musical partner and cowriter on "Do Ya Wanna Funk." Sarah became an in-demand session singer, working with acts like the O'Jays, David Johansen, Bo Diddley, Ronnie Wood, Jellybean, and many others. She sang a gorgeous duet with Nile Rodgers on "My Love Song for You," from the underrated *Adventures in the Land of the Good Groove*. Her solo LP on Manhattan Records, *You're All I Need*, was another LP that fell through the promotion net. A gospel-infused dance music single was released in 2012, "Hold On (He'll Be Right There)," produced by Jason King and Gavin Bradley.

Sarah Dash and Keith Richards maintained their connection from the days when Patti LaBelle and the Bluebelles opened for the Rolling Stones' second US tour. Keith asked Sarah to sing backing vocals on his tour in 1988, and their ongoing musical relationship saw Sarah adding backing vocals to the Stones' *Steel Wheels* LP, as well as dueting with Keith on "Make No Mistake" and "Rockawhile" on Keith's *Talk Is Cheap* LP. Sarah lends vocals and is credited as cowriter on the Richards track "Bodytalks." Sarah also sang on Keith's 2015 LP, *Crosseyed Heart*, and has toured with him to support his solo career with his band, the X-Pensive Winos. According to Keith's memoir, Sarah's live lead vocal on "Time Is on My Side" is his favorite version of the song.

Sarah headlined with the Teatro ZinZanni, and she

performs at various LGBTQ parades. She's working on a gospel album, continues to perform at venues with a more jazz-oriented set, and is working on her autobiography. She sits on several committees for the Grammys, serving in different capacities, and is currently a trustee for the newly formed New Jersey Capital Philharmonic Orchestra. She designs music courses for children and for the College of New Jersey's program "Trenton Makes Music." Sarah was appointed Trenton's music ambassador in 2017, and she advocates for musicians' rights with the Recording Academy on Capitol Hill.

In 1995, Sarah reunited with Patti LaBelle and Nona Hendryx to record the dance track "Turn It Out" for the film *To Wong Foo, Thanks for Everything! Julie Newmar.* Set loose on dance floors by master mixers Frankie Knuckles and Shep Pettibone, the track sailed to number one on the dance charts, proving Labelle's staying power as a sonic force to contend with. (Patti throws down a RuPaul-worthy instructional at the end of the song, which became their first charted hit in nineteen years.)

Labelle reunited in 2008 for a long-awaited suite of songs called *Back to Now*, released on Verve/Universal one month before Barack Obama was elected as POTUS. Unfortunately the label Universal Music TV hardly publicized their eight-city tour in support of the LP; hence, many fans weren't aware of the shows, but those fans and critics in the know were in heaven. Obama's election indicated a new day for America, and Labelle was back together to celebrate the moment. When Labelle took the stage at the Apollo Theater after a thirty-two-year absence, pandemonium ensued. Their thrilling blend was in full effect, rekindled anew as a sexy, world-wise maturity. Hoodwinking time, Sarah, Nona, and Patti looked fab, dressed in jewel-toned silks and still working feathers woven into headdresses fit for our Afronautic queens.

When I asked about *Back to Now*, Nona explained, "It's basically a continuation from where we stopped off." Nona had written two of the songs for the LP meant to follow *Chameleon* in 1977. Sexy woo songs and political sensibilities continue on this disc, with the funk swamp of "Candlelight," produced by Lenny Kravitz (the standout track for me), and "System," where Sarah, Patti, and Nona trade off lead vocal lines.

When I asked Lenny what it was like to work with the reunited Labelle, he said,

I wanted to have them sound like they did, but fresh, with new songs. I wanted it to be organic. All real instruments, string arrangements, the whole nine. I fell in love with the songs I was presented ["Superlover," "System," and "Candlelight"]. Watching and listening to them find their blend around one microphone was absolutely astonishing. I don't know how long it had been since they were in the studio together, but the blend was perfection. It was really beautiful to experience. But of course, getting the right vocal sound for Patti took a lot of work because she was just blowing out microphones and the recording console. The power in her vocal is ridiculously strong and when she goes, she goes.

"Superlover" is a cowrite by Nona, Patti, and Sarah, a slow dance to pitch the woo to. Completing this ballad's retro feel, Lenny tags the first lyric lines of the chorus with a melodic horn riff reminiscent of 1970s TV show themes (*M*A*S*H* comes to mind), giving that extra cozy feeling, a little lagniappe to the over-sixty set who grew up with Labelle. I mentioned this to Lenny, and he laughed: "That's funny, because those horn lines are slightly cheesy, but they work. I love television theme songs from the '60s and '70s. They had the best writers, producers, musicians, and arrangers creating them."

Wyclef Jean produced and auto-tuned Labelle's voices on the track "Roll Out," possibly in a bid to up-rez their act for a contemporary breed of listeners who prefer their voices robotic. But auto-tune isn't for vocal royalty; it's for pretty faces that can't hit and hold a clean pitch. At least it *was*, until it became an overused cliché. "Tears for the World" is true to the title, an impassioned plea for empathy in a NOLA sway and groove. Written by Patti with Gamble and Huff, the choir sings the coda out: "Have mercy on the world." "Dear Rosa" is a sonic catafalque to Rosa Parks, penned by Nona. "How Long" questions when nature will finally give up on us: "How long—before the oceans and the rivers run dry? How long—until the moon and the sun refuse to shine?" Nona testifies on the rock-gospel track "The Truth Will Set You Free," and it sure sounds like the Labelle women might be singing to each other on the ballad "Without You in My Life."

The LP includes a previously unreleased recording of Cole Porter's "Miss Otis Regrets," with an old touring buddy, the Who's Keith Moon, on drums and a dramatic piano reading of the song by Nicky Hopkins (Stones, Beatles, Kinks, Who). Labelle's version of this classic is a stunner. And for their beloved fan base, a bonus track: their cover of Sylvester's "You Make Me Feel (Mighty Real)." The song opens with a whispered invitation from Patti: "Do you wanna funk with me?" Twist my arm, Ms. Patti.

Labelle's music and rock star showmanship pointed the way to Afrofuturist possibilities in the arts, to Afropunk and all manner of sonic female individuations. They opened a portal for female artists to step through, giving courage to those creating their own hyper-singular material. Artists like Grace Jones, Beyoncé, Madonna, Meshell Ndegeocello, En Vogue, TLC, Missy Elliott, Queen Latifah, Destiny's Child, Pink, Janelle Monáe, and Lady Gaga owe a debt to progenitors Labelle. Nelly sampled "Isn't It a Shame" for his hit "My Place," and Kanye West took a piece of their recording of "You'll Never Walk Alone" for his song "Homecoming." Lee Daniels included Labelle recordings as the perfect underscore to scenes in his Academy Award–nominated film *Precious*. Baz Luhrmann included "Lady Marmalade" in his opus *Moulin Rouge!*

Covered by Christina Aguilera, Lil' Kim, Pink, and Mýa, the song reprised its number one spot on the *Billboard* pop charts twenty-seven years after Labelle's version.

Nona speaks to their influence: "We're very aware of the children that have to come after us and [will] live in this world 100 years from now. I want the children then to understand there were people here who were aware of the problems." I spoke with the brilliant musician and singer Gail Ann Dorsey (David Bowie's longtime bassist, currently with Lenny Kravitz's band) and asked whether she felt Labelle had influenced her own path. She replied,

> If you put on a big-ass pair of headphones, sit back, close your eyes, and crank the *Nightbirds*, or *Chameleon* album, or *It's Gonna Take a Miracle* with Laura Nyro, you will experience the deepest, purest meaning of the *power of the human voice* from three of the most passionate, powerful, and uniquely gifted singers you will ever hear. Beyond inspiration, their sound was about transformation. Impossible not to be moved to the core. I can exist in the world today as a Black female musician with confidence, and the courage to be myself and speak from the heart, because Labelle and their music showed me the way.

Collectively and individually, Labelle's recordings are testaments to the power of music: the scope and breadth of our deepest, most profound sentiments expressed through the beauty of the human voice.

I remember listening to Labelle in NYC when AIDS began its reign of terror. In the late 1970s, the gay community turned the city's decay into a dance palace, but our euphoria gave way to dread in the early '80s. Several of Labelle's collaborators were taken by the disease. Too many gay men, sick and frightened, broken by the shame and the physical pain the virus inflicted so monstrously. So many lives, too beautiful to face death's reckoning so young. Labelle recordings were precious jewels to the queer community—the ones taken and the ones left to tell the story. Their records remain cherished by a queer community decimated by the epidemic, a community desperately needing love in the heaping doses Labelle's music provided.

When Labelle relinquished the masks of 1950s and '60s female propriety and embraced their true feelings and imaginations, they enacted the cosmic dance of Shiva/Shakti as spacegirl, one foot stomping down to destroy the girl-group paradigm of assimilation, the other foot raised in creation of the new: a look, a fierce beat, and a siren song of women as free beings embracing the ecstatic. Their voices tore through the restraints binding the longing of so many girls and women, people of color, queer outsiders, and the lonely. All those longing to be acknowledged. Loved. Celebrated.

Today the corporate music business produces synthesized hit songs more akin to sonic algorithms than actual music. In our digital-screen age, where every nuance of a singer's recorded emotion must be tuned, squeezed, and compressed into oblivion, the analog majesty of Labelle's vocal blend has no equal; their voices, wild and brave on every piece of tape they ever graced with notes. These women know a secret. It's the recipe of the musical sorceress: how to sing the dark into light. The unraveling of womankind's buried musical history is just beginning, and clearly, it is ours for the telling or it won't be told. We snatch the hauntology of the ghost girl and dress her in the female star-body, where Toni Morrison's revenant Beloved meets that child locked in the basement of Ursula K. Le Guin's "The Ones Who Walk Away from Omelas." They will approach one another with wonder. As Labelle songs introduce them to an infinite capacity for joy, together, they'll dance.

In Labelle's legacy, we discover the power of music to lift us into a new dimension, where the view is astonishing, where music can hold hearts, erase divisions, and transform culture. Labelle created a liberation theology of music. They did not wait for permission. Their music continues to demand the powers that be to "take their feet off our necks,"[6] so that we can fly.

EPILOGUE

If one knew what rhythm is needed for a particular
individual in their trouble and despair, what tone is
needed, and to what tone that person's soul should be
raised, then one could heal a person with music.

HAZRAT INAYAT KHAN

In the spirit of sonic healing and why music matters, I've
saved one Labelle song for last: "Nightbird." The song of
the night bird captures a particular tristesse, a loneliness
that walks hand in hand with the sacrifices a woman has to
make, and the extraordinary will it takes to survive, intact.
The cost of being brave as a woman can be immeasurable,
but in that cost is an opening, again and again, to grace.

The flight of a woman's inner life is portrayed in the
song "Nightbird": how imagination and music can transform sorrow into transcendence, no matter how bitter-
sweet. The line Patti breaks out, "She feeds the fire for the
flame," gives voice to a woman unafraid to take a chance
for the sake of chance, no matter the consequence. When
asked about the song's inspiration, Nona says she wrote it
in tribute to Janis Joplin after reading an exploitive biography written by one of Joplin's lovers.

There's another layer to "Nightbird." I must go dark
here in order to excavate the light of the song's healing.

I return to Patti talking in her memoir of being sexually abused as a child, which is a hard story to read and to hear. And yet we desperately need to know these stories so we don't feel alone with our own. A slogan of activists during the AIDS pandemic, SILENCE = DEATH, is just as applicable to the silence of women over too many centuries. Silence feeds shame. The shame abused children carry is hard to shake. I can't say I know many women who have not been sexually or violently abused, and men are by no means excluded from experiencing this violence. But the trauma falls most heavily on women and girls. I thank Patti for her vulnerability in telling that story.

I have a story to tell.

A girl of thirteen ran away from a foster home and, seeking shelter, met a Vietnam vet in a public square. He seemed kind, offering her a place to stay at what he described as a hippie commune. His kindness was a ruse, and the girl became his hostage. He kept her locked in a room for three days with a loaded gun held to her temple, using her body, feeding off her fear. This is what feeds rape at its core: the victim's fear brings power to the soul killer, to the man who feels he has no power in the world aside from terrorizing the weaker—in this case, a child. After several moments of terror and abuse, the girl thought to herself, *If I live through this I will never ever be afraid of anything again.* After three days of terror and abuse, the man went out for supplies, and while he was away, two women broke through the door's lock and liberated the girl.

The girl grew and survived by burying the violation deep in her consciousness where the ugliest secrets sleep. She did not dare think of it for many years until she heard a song, like a lullaby, called "Nightbird." The song tripped a switch on her memory, taking her back to the hours when she rose above the bed and hovered there in the dark, watching her body below . . . that child beneath the man and his gun, and she, floating above, utterly detached and free. As if winged. On her way to a place where one day she would learn to transform the pain into something brave, and maybe beautiful. "Released, relived, just for the day . . . it's a nightbird's way . . ."

In an autoscopic experience, a traumatized person disassociates so severely that a split occurs between the physical body and the mind suffering the trauma. It feels as if you've died painlessly, like you've just up and walked out of your body while the violence is happening . . . like Sophia Nahli Allison's runaway Igbo slaves, or Solomon's flight in Toni Morrison's *Song of Solomon*, published in 1977, the year Labelle disbanded. I wonder if Morrison listened to Labelle while she was teaching Solomon how to fly, or when she created a character named Pilate; parts witch, pirate, and bird, Pilate flew while never leaving the ground. Did Pilate's creator know the song of the "Nightbird"? Flight is ritual, is sacred transport for Labelle, who sang of intergalactic sky creatures. Of spacegirls destined for a star-blessed Other.

Autoscopy creates an eerie feeling of flight, into space,

into peace. Music can do this too; can move the violated body and heart *from terror to transcendence*, a phrase from the beautiful mind of the writer Maria Popova. The tension of the etheric cord tying the girl of thirteen to her remembered violation was eased, unwound by the love contained *in a song*—one that begins with the tenderness of a lullaby and builds to a righteous gospel choir, driving the night bird to fly on toward liberty. Immersed inside that song of flight, the girl, then a young woman, felt able to relive, and then to release. Her wound, soothed, for the very first time.

Give a woman a mask, and its truth will set her free.

There's a magical elixir in the hearts of healers that, once conjured into music, becomes as sacred as prayer. "Labelle brought the love, the joy," says Nikki Giovanni. A love ever revolving, Labelle spin their messages in immortal musical time. Open the windows. Break some glass if you have to, and *listen*.

ACKNOWLEDGMENTS

Thanks to Evelyn McDonnell: for mentoring me into authorship as well as her keen editorial eye and for her unwavering support for women who rock. Big gratitude to my editor, Casey Kittrell, for shepherding me through the process of making this book and for helping abate my terror over writing for an academic press. Thanks to the team at UT Press for the opportunity and the guidance. Thanks to my rock, Natalie Hill, for the ongoing friendship and support. To the following people, thank you for your generosity of memory, insight, and time: Nikki Giovanni, Vicki Wickham, Nona Hendryx, Sarah Dash, Lenny Kravitz, Dawn Silva, Gayle Wald, Michael Gonzalez, Anonymous, and Gail Ann Dorsey. Thanks to all the scholars, authors, and journalists (listed in sources) whose work made mine a thrilling journey of discovery. And thank you Patti, Nona, and Sarah for sharing your tremendous gifts with us. Your music continues to make the world a better place.

NOTES

1. Church

1. The publishing company Labelle created for the majority of their original songs is called Gospel Birds.
2. Hans Jenny, *Cymatics: A Study of Wave Phenomena and Vibration* (n.p.: MACROmedia, 2001).
3. Stephon Alexander, *The Jazz of Physics: The Secret Link between Music and the Structure of the Universe* (New York: Basic Books, 2016).
4. Stephen W. Porges and Deb Dana, eds., *Clinical Applications of the Polyvagal Theory: The Emergence of Polyvagal-Informed Therapies* (New York: W. W. Norton, 2018).
5. Leon Petchkovsky, Kristin Robertson-Gillam, Juri Kropotov, and Michael Petchkovsky, "Using QEEG Parameters (Asymmetry, Coherence, and P3a Novelty Response) to Track Improvement in Depression after Choir Therapy," *Advances in Mental Health* 11, no. 3 (2013): 257–267.
6. Nona Hendryx, interview by the author.
7. Karen Grigsby Bates, "Olivia Butler: Writing Herself into the Story," NPR, *Morning Edition*, July 10, 2017, https://www.npr.org/sections/codeswitch/2017/07/10/535879364/octavia-butler-writing-herself-into-the-story.
8. Sarah Dash, interview by the author.
9. Morgan Neville, dir., *20 Feet from Stardom*, 2013.
10. "The Journey of Patti LaBelle (2001)," YouTube video, uploaded by reelblack, May 11, 2019, https://www.youtube.com/watch?v=NTDTEElVL90.
11. Mark Anthony Neal, "More Than Chitlins on the Chitlin' Circuit," *MadameNoire*, August 24, 2011, https://madamenoire.com/69929/more-than-chitlins-on-the-chitlin-circuit/.
12. "Patti LaBelle - Interview - 3/20/1986 - Unknown (Official)," YouTube video, uploaded by Docs&Interviews on MV, September 25, 2014, https://www.youtube.com/watch?v=CPDQsl0SSOk.

2. Regarding "Mr. Lee"

1. Alan Betrock, *Girl Groups: The Story of a Sound* (New York: Delilah Books, 1982).

2. Benjamin Turner and Gabe Turner, dirs., *Hitsville: The Making of Motown* (2019).

3. "Sojourner Truth, 'I Sell the Shadow to Support the Substance,'" Metropolitan Museum of Art, n.d., https://www.metmuseum.org/art /collection/search/301989.

4. "The Pope Sisters - First Black Girl Group," YouTube video, uploaded by MusicandDancing4Ever, August 26, 2016, https://www .youtube.com/watch?v=SBVFwmJssYc.

3. Sweethearts of the Apollo

1. Luther Vandross, interview, in "Patti Labelle Biography - Intimate Portrait Part 1/5," YouTube video, uploaded by PattiBiography, April 23, 2008, https://www.youtube.com/watch?v=rRm1RC6t0YE.

2. Nona Hendryx, interview, in Michael Glitz, "Exclusive: Nona Hendryx Speaks Out!," *HuffPost*, January 15, 2009, https://www .huffpost.com/entry/huffpo-exclusive-labelles_b_151233.

3. Simon Napier-Bell, *Black Vinyl, White Powder* (London: Ebury, 2001).

4. Charlotte Heathcote, "Vicki Wickham Interview: We Put on a Good Show," *Express*, May 30, 2010, https://www.express.co.uk /entertainment/music/178089/Vicki-Wickham-interview-We-put -on-a-good-show.

5. "Patti Labelle and the Bluebelles - All or Nothing (Rare Clip 1966)," YouTube video, uploaded by ILMJXXX, December 23, 2017, https:// www.youtube.com/watch?v=1XHMBKhlY9Y.

6. Patti LaBelle, with Laura B. Randolph, *Don't Block the Blessings: Revelations of a Lifetime* (New York: Riverhead Books, 1996).

4. *Ready Steady Go!*

1. "Patti Labelle 1975 Interview with Vicki Wickham, Nona Hendryx and Sarah Dash," YouTube video, uploaded by fred fishers, January 6, 2017, https://www.youtube.com/watch?v=i8dYogrrh2s.

2. Francis Hitching, "Ready, Steady, Goes: Celebrating the Life of Ready, Steady, Go! as It Finishes at the End of 1966," Transdiffusion's Rediffusion, London, July 24, 2018, http://rediffusion.london/ready-steady-goes.

3. Gayle Wald, "Nowhere to Run: Girl Group Transnationalism" (paper, MoPop Pop Conference, Museum of Pop Culture, Seattle, WA, April 21, 2017).

4. "Dusty Springfield Bravely Comes Out as Bisexual in 'The Evening Standard,' 1970," *Dangerous Minds*, January 3, 2014, https://dangerousminds.net/comments/dusty_springfield_bravely_comes_out_as_bisexual_in_the_evening_standard_197.

5. Penny Valentine and Vicki Wickham, *Dancing with Demons: The Authorized Biography of Dusty Springfield* (New York: St. Martin's, 2000).

6. Caroline Sullivan, "Ready, Vicki, Go," *Guardian*, November 29, 1999, https://www.theguardian.com/culture/1999/nov/30/artsfeatures1.

5. Pyrotechnic Gospel Punk

1. Quoted in Stanislas Klossowski de Rola, *The Golden Game: Alchemical Engravings of the Seventeenth Century* (London: Thames and Hudson, 1997).

2. "Patti Labelle Biography - Intimate Portrait Part 2/5," YouTube video, uploaded by PattiBiography, April 23, 2008, https://www.youtube.com/watch?v=QfG_8DcuACo.

3. Audre Lorde, *Sister Outsider: Essays and Speeches* (n.p.: Crossing, 1984).

6. Campanology

1. Mark Anthony Neal, *Songs in the Key of Black Life: A Rhythm and Blues Nation* (London: Routledge, 2003).

2. Federico García Lorca, *Deep Song and Other Prose* (New York: New Directions, 1980).

3. René Descartes, *The Passions of the Soul* (Indianapolis, IN: Hackett, 1989).

4. "Laura Nyro 1971 Carnegie Hall," YouTube video, uploaded by Den Knee, April 8, 2013, https://www.youtube.com/watch?v=n3lgYdasCPc.

7. Revolution, Televised

1. Timothy Greenfield-Sanders, dir., *Toni Morrison: The Pieces I Am* (2019).
2. "Brian Eno on Basic Income," YouTube video, uploaded by Basic Income UK, January 11, 2016, https://www.youtube.com/watch?v= qkD7JBspgas.
3. "James Baldwin and Nikki Giovanni, a Conversation [FULL]," YouTube video, uploaded by thepostarchive, January 16, 2019, https:// www.youtube.com/watch?v=eZmBy7C9gHQ.
4. "LaBelle Live on Soul! 1972 (Nona Hendryx, Sarah Dash, and Patti LaBelle)," YouTube video, uploaded by Luther Carter IV, January 9, 2018, https://www.youtube.com/watch?v=nq5xBCkCLaM.
5. Patti LaBelle and Laura Randolph Lancaster, *Patti's Pearls: Lessons in Living Genuinely, Joyfully, Generously* (New York: Grand Central, 2001).
6. Wesley Morris, "For Centuries, Black Music, Forged in Bondage, Has Been the Sound of Complete Artistic Freedom; No Wonder Everybody Is Always Stealing It," *New York Times Magazine*, August 14, 2019, https:// www.nytimes.com/interactive/2019/08/14/magazine/music-black -culture-appropriation.html.

8. Afronauticfuturisticfunkadivalicious

1. Nickie Roberts, *Whores in History: Prostitution in Western Society* (New York: HarperCollins, 1993).
2. "Voulez-vous coucher avec moi . . . John Lennon Covers Labelle," YouTube video, uploaded by In The Life of . . . The Beatles, May 24, 2018, https://www.youtube.com/watch?v=MP4l80dVuO0.
3. Audre Lorde, "The Erotic as Power," in *Sister Outsider* (New York: Random House, 1984).
4. "Nona Hendryx Interview Segment on Videowave," YouTube video, uploaded by Videowave Music, November 26, 2013, https://www .youtube.com/watch?v=7V0ENJQwSto.

9. Mothers of Reinvention

1. Patti Labelle, interview, in Rick Owens, *Legaspi* (New York: Rizzoli, 2019).
2. Sarah Dash, interview by the author.

3. Nona Hendryx, interview by the author.
4. Nona Hendryx, interview by the author.
5. Art Harris, interview with Labelle, *Rolling Stone*, July 3, 1975.
6. Ann Powers, "Labelle Was Always More Than a 'Lady,'" *Los Angeles Times*, October 12, 2008, http://articles.latimes.com/2008/oct/12/entertainment/ca-labelle12.
7. Art Harris, interview with Labelle, *Rolling Stone*, July 3, 1975.
8. Dawn Silva, interview by the author.
9. Rick Owens, *Legaspi* (New York: Rizzoli, 2019).
10. Karu F. Daniels, "Nona Hendryx to Bring Afrofuturism Performance to Metropolitan Museum of Art with Special Sun Ra Tribute," *New York Daily News*, February 27, 2020, https://www.nydailynews.com/snyde/ny-nona-hendryx-sun-ra-tribute-afrofuturism-metropolitan-museum-harlem-20200227-exv6yqunerbwpctweaukwl2iem-story.html.

10. An Epic Triptych

1. "Patti Labelle Biography - Intimate Portrait Part 3/5," YouTube video, uploaded by PattiBiography, April 23, 2008, https://www.youtube.com/watch?v=TPgd25juF-s.
2. Thelma "Butterfly" McQueen played the maid Prissy in *Gone with the Wind*. Neither McQueen nor Hattie McDaniel (who won the Oscar for her supporting role in the film as Mammy) were allowed to attend the film premiere or the Oscars because of their race.
3. Luther Vandross, interview, in "Patti Labelle Biography—Intimate Portrait Part 3/5," YouTube video, uploaded by PattiBiography, April 23, 2008, https://www.youtube.com/watch?v=TPgd25juF-s.
4. José Esteban Muñoz, *Cruising Utopia: The Then and There of Queer Futurity* (New York: New York University Press, 2009).

11. Apotheosis

1. Caroline Sullivan, "Patti LaBelle: 'Lady Marmalade? We Thought It Was Just About a Woman Walking Down the Street,'" *Guardian*, November 12, 2015, https://www.theguardian.com/culture/2015/nov/12/patti-labelle-lady-marmalade-woman-walking-down-street.

2. Marcus James Dixon, "Patti LaBelle ('The Masked Singer' Flower)," *GoldDerby*, November 21, 2019, https://www.goldderby.com/article /2019/patti-labelle-the-masked-singer-flower-exit-interview-video/.

3. Chris Franz, *Remain in Love: Talking Heads, Tom Tom Club, Tina* (New York: St. Martin's, 2020).

4. Pat Place, interview by the author.

5. Taylor Hosking, "Nona Hendryx Takes Over the Met's Temple of Dendur in the Ultimate Tribute to Sun Ra," *Observer*, February 27, 2020, https://observer.com/2020/02/nona-hendryx-sun-ra-tribute -takes-over-met-temple-of-dendur/.

6. A "Notorious RBG" quote from the documentary on Ruth Bader Ginsburg directed by Betsy West and Julie Cohen: "I ask no favor for my sex; all I ask of our brethren is that they take their feet off our necks."

SOURCES

"#AFTVNYC Episode 69: The Nona Hendryx Interview (YouTube Extended)." YouTube video, uploaded by THE ARTISTS FORUM, April 5, 2016. https://www.youtube.com/watch?v=QZ8CKG4dBqA.

Alexander, Stephon. *The Jazz of Physics: The Secret Link between Music and the Structure of the Universe*. New York: Basic Books, 2016.

Allison, Sophia Nahli. "Revisiting the Legend of Flying Africans." *New Yorker*, March 7, 2019. https://www.newyorker.com/culture/culture-desk/revisiting-the-legend-of-flying-africans.

Alpert, Steve, dir. *Girl Groups: Story of a Sound*. 1983.

Bates, Karen Grigsby. "Octavia Butler: Writing Herself into the Story." NPR, *Morning Edition*, July 10, 2017. https://www.npr.org/sections/codeswitch/2017/07/10/535879364/octavia-butler-writing-herself-into-the-story.

Betrock, Alan. *Girl Groups: The Story of a Sound*. New York: Delilah Books, 1982.

Bogdan, Deanne. "Music, McLuhan, Modality: Musical Experience From 'Extreme Occasion' to 'Alchemy.'" *Media Tropes* 1 (2008): 71–101.

"Brian Eno on Basic Income." YouTube video, uploaded by Basic Income UK, January 11, 2016. https://www.youtube.com/watch?v=qkD7JBspgas.

Butler, Octavia. "'Devil Girl from Mars': Why I Write Science Fiction." Transcript of talk given on February 19, 1998. MIT Black History, n.d. https://www.blackhistory.mit.edu/archive/transcript-devil-girl-mars-why-i-write-science-fiction-octavia-butler-1998.

Byrne, David. *How Music Works*. San Francisco: McSweeney's Books, 2012.

Davis, Angela Y. *Women, Race and Class*. New York: Vintage Books, 1983.

Dery, Mark. "Black to the Future: Afro-Futurism 1.0." Rumori, n.d. http://www.detritus.net/contact/rumori/200211/0319.html.

Descartes, René. *The Passions of the Soul*. Indianapolis, IN: Hackett, 1989.

Dixon, Marcus James. "Patti LaBelle ('The Masked Singer' Flower)."

GoldDerby, November 21, 2019. https://www.goldderby.com/article/2019/patti-labelle-the-masked-singer-flower-exit-interview-video/.

Douglas, Susan J. *Where the Girls Are: Growing Up Female with the Mass Media*. New York: Three Rivers, 1994.

Echols, Alice. *Hot Stuff: Disco and the Remaking of American Culture*. New York: W. W. Norton, 2010.

Ellison, Ralph. "Change the Joke and Slip the Yoke." In *Shadow and Act*, 45–59. New York: Vintage International, 1995.

Eshun, Kodwo. *More Brilliant Than the Sun: Adventures in Sonic Fiction*. London: Quartet Books, 1998.

Fisher, Mark. *Ghosts of My Life: Writings on Depression, Hauntology and Lost Futures*. Hants, UK: Zero Books, 2014.

Franz, Chris. *Remain in Love: Talking Heads, Tom Tom Club, Tina*. New York: St. Martin's, 2020.

Giovanni, Nikki. *Black Feeling, Black Talk, Black Judgement*. New York: William Morrow, 1968.

Glitz, Michael. "Exclusive: Nona Hendryx Speaks Out!" *HuffPost*, January 15, 2009. https://www.huffpost.com/entry/huffpo-exclusive-labelles_b_151233.

"Going Black: The Legacy of Philly Soul Radio (One Hour Special)." PRX, January 6, 2014. https://beta.prx.org/stories/108596-going-black-the-legacy-of-philly-soul-radio-one.

"Golden Age of Black Radio - Part 2: Deejays." Google Arts and Culture exhibit, Indiana University Archives of African American Music and Culture, n.d. https://artsandculture.google.com/exhibit/tQKCWDGh2AvJJw.

Greenfield-Sanders, Timothy, dir. *Toni Morrison: The Pieces I Am*. Magnolia Pictures, 2019.

Gulla, Bob. *Icons of R&B and Soul: An Encyclopedia of the Artists Who Revolutionized Rhythm*. Vol. 1. Westport, CT: Greenwood, 2008.

Hall, Manly P. *The Therapeutic Value of Music*. Los Angeles: Philosophical Research Society, 1982.

Harris, Art. Interview with Labelle. *Rolling Stone*, July 3, 1975.

Heathcote, Charlotte. "Vicki Wickham Interview: We Put on a Good Show." *Express*, May 30, 2010. https://www.express.co.uk

/entertainment/music/178089/Vicki-Wickham-interview-We-put-on
-a-good-show.

Hitching, Francis. "Ready, Steady, Goes: Celebrating the Life of Ready,
Steady, Go! as It Finishes at the End of 1966." Transdiffusion's
Rediffusion, London, July 24, 2018. http://rediffusion.london/ready
-steady-goes.

hooks, bell. *All About Love*. New York: HarperCollins, 2001.

———. *Black Looks: Race and Representation*. Boston: South End, 1987.

Hosking, Taylor. "Nona Hendryx Takes Over the Met's Temple of Dendur
in the Ultimate Tribute to Sun Ra." *Observer*, February 27, 2020. https://
observer.com/2020/02/nona-hendryx-sun-ra-tribute-takes-over-met
-temple-of-dendur/.

Iton, Richard. *In Search of the Black Fantastic: Politics and Popular Culture in the
Post–Civil Rights Era*. New York: Oxford University Press, 2008.

James, Marlon. *The Book of Night Women*. New York: Riverhead Books,
2009.

"James Baldwin and Nikki Giovanni, a Conversation [FULL]." YouTube
video, uploaded by thepostarchive, January 16, 2019. https://www
.youtube.com/watch?v=eZmBy7C9gHQ.

Jenny, Hans. *Cymatics: A Study of Wave Phenomena and Vibration*. N.p.:
MACROmedia, 2001.

"John Lennon Lady Marmalade." YouTube video, uploaded by Serge
Francoeur, October 4, 2014. https://www.youtube.com/watch?v=
ZOYVetEcKak.

"The Journey of Patti LaBelle (2001)." YouTube video, uploaded by
reelblack, May 11, 2019. https://www.youtube.com/watch?v=
NTDTEElVL90.

Khan, Hazrat Inayat. *The Mysticism of Sound and Music: The Sufi Teaching of
Hazrat Inayat Khan*. Rev. ed. Boston: Shambhala, 1996.

LaBelle, Patti, with Laura B. Randolph. *Don't Block the Blessings: Revelations
of a Lifetime*. New York: Riverhead Books, 1996.

LaBelle, Patti, and Laura Randolph Lancaster. *Patti's Pearls: Lessons in
Living Genuinely, Joyfully, Generously*. New York: Grand Central, 2001.

"LaBelle Live on Soul! 1972 (Nona Hendryx, Sarah Dash, and Patti
LaBelle)." YouTube video, uploaded by Luther Carter IV, January 9,
2018. https://www.youtube.com/watch?v=nq5xBCkCLaM.

"Larry LeGaspi Archive." Instagram album by gofreemoonstone, n.d. https://www.instagram.com/gofreemoonstone/?hl=en.

Lask, Thomas. "Soul Festival: A Cool Nikki Giovanni Reads Poetry." *New York Times*, July 26, 1972. https://www.nytimes.com/1972/07/26/archives/soul-festival-a-cool-nikki-giovanni-reads-poetry.html.

"Laura Nyro 1971 Carnegie Hall." YouTube video, uploaded by Den Knee, April 8, 2013. https://www.youtube.com/watch?v=n3lgYdasCPc.

Lauterbach, Preston. *The Chitlin' Circuit and the Road to Rock 'n' Roll.* New York: W. W. Norton, 2011.

Ledbetter, Les. "Sunday Is Soul Day at Lincoln Center." *New York Times*, July 21, 1972. https://www.nytimes.com/1972/07/21/archives/sunday-is-soul-day-at-lincoln-center.html.

Le Guin, Ursula K. *The Unreal and the Real: Where on Earth; Selected Stories Volume One.* London: Gollancz, 2012.

Lorca, Federico García. *Deep Song and Other Prose.* New York: New Directions, 1980.

Lorde, Audre. *Sister Outsider: Essays and Speeches.* N.p.: Crossing, 1984.

Mahon, Maureen. *The Right to Rock: The Black Rock Coalition and the Cultural Politics of Race.* Durham, NC: Duke University Press, 2004.

Manji, Irshad. *Don't Label Me: An Incredible Conversation for Divided Times.* New York: St. Martin's, 2019.

McDonnell, Evelyn, ed. *Women Who Rock: Bessie to Beyoncé, Girl Groups to Riot Grrrl.* New York: Black Dog and Leventhal, 2018.

Morris, Wesley. "For Centuries, Black Music, Forged in Bondage, Has Been the Sound of Complete Artistic Freedom; No Wonder Everybody Is Always Stealing It." *New York Times Magazine*, August 14, 2019. https://www.nytimes.com/interactive/2019/08/14/magazine/music-black-culture-appropriation.html.

Morrison, Toni. *Beloved.* New York: Vintage Books, 1987.

———. *Song of Solomon.* New York: Alfred A. Knopf, 1977.

———. *The Source of Self-Regard: Selected Essays, Speeches, and Meditations.* New York: Alfred A. Knopf, 2019.

Muñoz, José Esteban. *Cruising Utopia: The Then and There of Queer Futurity.* New York: New York University Press, 2009.

Napier-Bell, Simon. *Black Vinyl, White Powder.* London: Ebury, 2001.

Neafsey, John. *A Sacred Voice Is Calling: Personal Vocation and Social*

Conscience. Maryknoll, NY: Orbis Books, 2015.

Neal, Larry. "The Black Arts Movement." In "Black Theatre." Special issue, *TDR/The Drama Review* 12, no. 4 (Summer, 1968): 28–39. http://nationalhumanitiescenter.org/pds/maai3/community/text8/blackartsmovement.pdf.

Neal, Mark Anthony. "More Than Chitlins on the Chitlin' Circuit." *MadameNoire*, August 24, 2011. https://madamenoire.com/69929/more-than-chitlins-on-the-chitlin-circuit/.

———. *Songs in the Key of Black Life: A Rhythm and Blues Nation*. London: Routledge, 2003.

Neville, Morgan, dir. *20 Feet from Stardom*. 2013.

"Nona Hendryx Interview Segment on Videowave." YouTube video, uploaded by Videowave Music, November 26, 2013. https://www.youtube.com/watch?v=7V0ENJQwSto.

Olsson, Göran, dir. *The Black Power Mixtape, 1967–1975*. 2011.

Owens, Rick. *Legaspi*. New York: Rizzoli, 2019.

"Patti Labelle and the Bluebelles - All or Nothing (Rare Clip 1966)." YouTube video, uploaded by ILMJXXX, December 23, 2017. https://www.youtube.com/watch?v=1XHMBKhlY9Y.

"Patti Labelle Biography - Intimate Portrait [Lifetime]." YouTube series in 5 parts, uploaded by PattiBiography, April 23, 2008. https://www.youtube.com/watch?v=rRm1RC6t0YE&list=RDrRm1RC6t0YE&start_radio=1&t=15; https://www.youtube.com/watch?v=QfG_8DcuACo; https://www.youtube.com/watch?v=TPgd25juF-s; https://www.youtube.com/watch?v=Yb22p-ykMbc; https://www.youtube.com/watch?v=zumlUP2f9m4.

"Patti LaBelle - Interview - 3/20/1986 - Unknown (Official)." YouTube video, uploaded by Docs&Interviews on MV, September 25, 2014. https://www.youtube.com/watch?v=CPDQsl0SSOk.

"Patti Labelle 1975 Interview with Vicki Wickham, Nona Hendryx and Sarah Dash." YouTube video, uploaded by fred fishers, January 6, 2017. https://www.youtube.com/watch?v=i8dYogrrh2s.

Petchkovsky, Leon, Kristin Robertson-Gillam, Juri Kropotov, and Michael Petchkovsky. "Using QEEG Parameters (Asymmetry, Coherence, and P3a Novelty Response) to Track Improvement in Depression after Choir Therapy." *Advances in Mental Health* 11, no. 3 (2013): 257–267.

"The Pope Sisters - First Black Girl Group." YouTube video, uploaded by MusicandDancing4Ever, August 26, 2016. https://www.youtube.com /watch?v=SBVFwmJssYc.

Popova, Maria. Figuring. New York: Pantheon Books, 2019.

Porges, Stephen W., and Deb Dana, eds. *Clinical Applications of the Polyvagal Theory: The Emergence of Polyvagal-Informed Therapies*. New York: W. W. Norton, 2018.

Powers, Ann. "Labelle Was Always More Than a 'Lady.'" *Los Angeles Times*, October 12, 2008. http://articles.latimes.com/2008/oct/12 /entertainment/ca-labelle12.

Roberts, Nickie. *Whores in History: Prostitution in Western Society*. New York: HarperCollins, 1993.

Rola, Stanislas Klossowski de. *The Golden Game: Alchemical Engravings of the Seventeenth Century*. London: Thames and Hudson, 1997.

Royster, Francesca. "Labelle: Funk, Feminism and the Politics of Flight and Fight." In "The Funk Issue." Special issue, *American Studies* 52, no. 4 (2013): 77–98.

———. *Sounding Like a No-No: Queer Sounds and Eccentric Acts in the Post-Soul Era*. Ann Arbor: University of Michigan Press, 2013.

Sacks, Oliver. *Musicophilia: Tales of Music and the Brain*. New York: Vintage Books, 2008.

"Sarah Dash: Change Had to Be Made." YouTube video, uploaded by Shefik presents Invocation, July 6, 2017. https://www.youtube.com/watch?v= _baoR-hFvKM.

"Sojourner Truth, 'I Sell the Shadow to Support the Substance.'" Metropolitan Museum of Art, n.d. https://www.metmuseum.org/art /collection/search/301989.

Spirit and Flesh. Nona Hendryx interview by Musa Jackson, n.d. https:// spiritandfleshmag.com/interviews/nona-hendryx/.

Sullivan, Caroline. "Patti LaBelle: 'Lady Marmalade? We Thought It Was Just About a Woman Walking Down the Street.'" *Guardian*, November 12, 2015. https://www.theguardian.com/culture/2015/nov/12/patti -labelle-lady-marmalade-woman-walking-down-street.

———. "Ready, Vicki, Go." *Guardian*, November 29, 1999. https://www .theguardian.com/culture/1999/nov/30/artsfeatures1.

Tenor, María. "Larry Legaspi, the Designer of the 70s Who Inspired the

Last Rick Owens Show." *Highxtar*, January 31, 2019. https://highxtar
.com/larry-legaspi-the-designer-of-the-70s-who-inspired-the-last-rick
-owens-show/?lang=en.

Thompson, Kathleen. "Girl Groups." *Oxford African American Studies Center*,
December 1, 2006. https://doi.org/10.1093/acref/9780195301731.013
.44167.

Trebay, Guy. "Rick Owens Offers Respect." *New York Times*, January 18,
2019. https://www.nytimes.com/2019/01/18/fashion/rick-owens-paris
-mens-fall-2019.html.

Turner, Benjamin, and Gabe Turner, dirs. *Hitsville: The Making of Motown*.
2019.

Valentine, Penny, and Vicki Wickham. *Dancing with Demons: The Authorized
Biography of Dusty Springfield*. New York: St. Martin's, 2000.

"Voulez-vous coucher avec moi . . . John Lennon Covers Labelle." YouTube
video, uploaded by In The Life of . . . The Beatles, May 24, 2018. https://
www.youtube.com/watch?v=MP4l80dVuO0.

Wald, Gayle. "The History of Soul! and Influence of Host Ellis Haizlip."
Thirteen, Broadcasting While Black, February 7, 2009. https://www
.thirteen.org/broadcastingwhileblack/uncategorized/the-history-of
-soul-and-influence-of-host-ellis-haizlip/.

———. *It's Been Beautiful: "Soul!" and Black Power Television*. Durham,
NC: Duke University Press, 2015.

———. "Nowhere to Run: Girl Group Transnationalism." Paper presented
at MoPop Pop Conference, Museum of Pop Culture, Seattle, WA, April
21, 2017.

Wallace, Michele. *Black Macho and the Myth of the Superwoman*. New York:
Dial, 1978.

Warwick, Jacqueline. *Girl Groups, Girl Culture: Popular Music and Identity in
the 1960s*. New York: Routledge, 2007.

Williams, Roger Ross, dir. *The Apollo*. 2019.

Womack, Ytasha L. *Afrofuturism: The World of Black Sci-Fi and Fantasy
Culture*. Chicago: Lawrence Hill Books, 2013.

Yaszek, Lisa. "Afrofuturism, Science Fiction, and the History of the Future."
Socialism and Democracy 20, no. 3 (November 2006): 41–60.